Youth Prints

To my grandson, Todd
a good reader +
future author!

Grand ma
Martha
E. Mumert

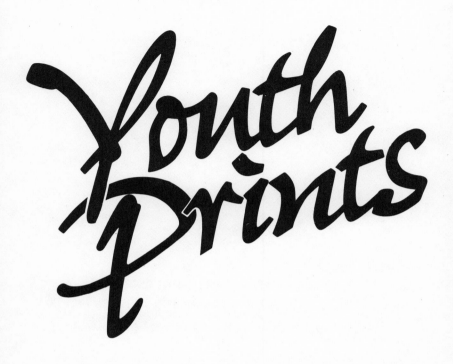

Youth Prints

E d i t e d   b y

NORMAN VINCENT PEALE

AUGSBURG Publishing House • Minneapolis

Library of Congress Cataloging-in-Publication Data

YOUTH PRINTS.

    1. Youth—Religious life.   2.Youth—Conduct of life.
I. Peale, Norman Vincent, 1898–
BV4531.2.Y67   1988   248.8'3   88-16786
ISBN 0-8066-2380-2

Manufactured in the U.S.A.   APH 10-7499

1 2 3 4 5 6 7 8 9 0 1 2 3 4 5 6 7 8 9

Contents

Editor's Preface

*I*t *has been said* ten thousand times that the future of this country rests in the hands of its young people. And that is certainly true. But it's a truth that some people seem to view with uneasiness or even alarm. Are our young people strong enough, they ask, and wise enough and disciplined enough to deal with the enormous problems that the future holds? Do they have the moral fiber, the religious values that the leaders of our country will need?

I wish all the skeptics and the doubters could read the book you are holding in your hands. Every item in it was written by a high school student. Each of these stories is true. Every one bears witness to the fact that a great many of our young people are wiser and more loving and more capable and just plain smarter than the generations that preceded them. It's a tremendously reassuring fact.

Some 20 years ago, hoping to encourage young people to express themselves, *Guideposts* magazine began offering scholarship prizes for high school juniors and seniors who sent in true stories showing how their religious faith had enriched their lives. The scholarship money could be used only for their college education. Last year some seven thousand manuscripts were entered in the Guideposts Youth Writing Contest. Some contestants won handsome scholarships, some won typewriters, all were really winners because they had the invaluable experience of putting words and thoughts on paper to the best of their ability. They became communicators, not just of ideas, but also of a sincere and glowing religious faith.

The title for this volume is very apt, I think. No two fingerprints are alike, but all are human. No two of these "youth print" stories are alike either, but all give heartening assurance that the future of our nation is in good hands.

In the Bible, the prophet Joel says, "Your young men will see visions" (2:28). Here assembled are some of the visions of our young people, boys and girls alike. I am proud to be able to introduce them to you—and you to them.

NORMAN VINCENT PEALE

Linda Diane Marshall

The Teacher Who Taught Me to Dream

*C*hildren, please repeat after me, 'I am only one, but I am one. I can't do everything, but I can do something. What I can do, I ought to do; and what I ought to do, by the grace of God, I will do!' "

That was my introduction to my eighth-grade homeroom teacher—the one special person who did most to make my faith grow. She was to be my homeroom teacher for the next three years and my English teacher for the eighth and eleventh grades.

Mrs. Carolyn Long was the smallest person in the room, but she dominated it. She smiled and we all were glad we had chosen that school. She walked, talked, and even seemed to eat too fast. She seemed to feel that time would run out before she taught us anything and that if it did the fault would be hers.

Yet there was no lack of patience with us. Instead she made each of us feel that we were special people without bestowing special favor upon anyone. She always found time to give each of us "his five minute" as she called it. None was neglected.

I came to her thoroughly convinced that I was never meant to be anybody of importance. I had long ago decided that no one cared and nothing mattered, so I existed from day to day without any thought of tomorrow. The distant future was beyond my conception. Drab and unhappy circumstances had stunted my growth, killed my faith, and left me floating on a directionless sea of time.

My home, I felt, was merely a place to go when school closed. I thought it a prison. My mother provided food and shelter for my body but really had little time for me. Separated from my father, she had full responsibility for my nine brothers and sisters. There just were too many other things which took her time. I never got my "five minute" with her as with Mrs. Long. We just never talked about the things I had on my mind.

I felt life was hopeless—and it was—until I met Mrs. Long, who kept nudging me with remarks like, "Use your mind, Linda, and free your body." "You can break out of the prison of your environment if you study hard and do your lessons every day." Or she would say, "You can be somebody if you want to be."

The Lord knows I wanted to be somebody.

She continued to admonish us daily with that devotional chant, "You are only one, but you are one. . . ."—meaning we ought to be proud of ourselves and if we weren't, we ought to have guts enough to do something about it. I tried not to listen, but I heard her. I tried to ignore what she meant, but I got the message, loud and clear. I told myself she was a fake, a too-good-to-be-true pretender, but she sounded so sincere. When I was on the verge of becoming a convert, I angrily denounced her for fussing all the time.

Then, one day she asked us to look out of the window and to write about whatever came into our minds as we

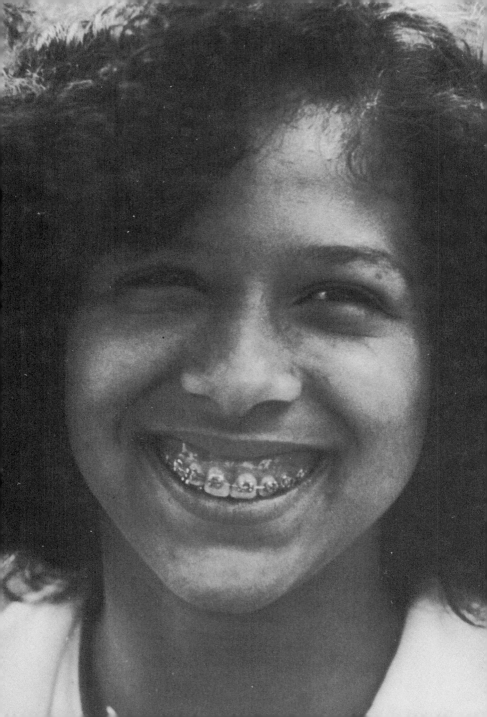

looked. It was a dark wintry day. I wrote a little poem about whispering leaves and the snow-kissed earth. She was ecstatic. One would have thought she had discovered another Shakespeare. I had never dared to show anyone my poetry before lest I be ridiculed. Her enthusiastic praise melted my sorrow and broke the dam of my resolution. I wrote all my themes in poetry that year.

She wouldn't accept dirty, incorrect work. We had to write it over until it was pretty and clean and errorless. Then basking in the glory of her smile we would pin it on the bulletin board. "See! Everyone can create beauty," she'd say, pointing to our themes, which, I must admit, did look beautiful. Sloppy work, she swore, would develop sloppy characters in us and that would blight our futures. Heaven forbid!

I could go on forever enumerating how this little, energetic, enthusiastic lady rekindled my faith in myself and my ability to fight against the odds; how she inspired me to a greater faith in God; how she helped me to believe in the innate goodness of my fellowman.

Slowly, I believed and slowly, believing changed me. I joined the student council. I accepted an invitation to appear on an assembly program. She helped me, encouraged me and was waiting to praise me when it was over; but sweeter than that was the thundering applause of my schoolmates who proved that she was right.

My sprouting wings continued to grow to full strength through my high school years. It was not always easy, but Mrs. Long was my radar, able to detect my wavering convictions, always encouraging, urging, and pointing the way.

"That's good, Linda, but you can do better," she would say and I would do better. If I stumbled she'd say, "You can't stop now, Linda," and I would try again.

With her help I have achieved confidence in my ability to face the future. I understand myself and my potential. I also understand the circumstances about my home.

My determination to find a way led me into business education and a trade. My dogged "do it well, if at all" training has gotten me a part-time job in one of the school offices and the confidence of my superiors. I dare to dream of a college degree, and I have the faith to believe that somehow, some way, I shall achieve it. After all, I am only one but I am one. I can't do everything, but I can do something. What I can do, I ought to do; and what I ought to do, by the grace of God, I will do! My most fervent prayer is that someday Mrs. Long will have cause to be really proud of me and that I shall be able to wrap the mantle of her faith around another child like myself.

Justin Fisher

The Prize
Worth Polishing

I had always felt that my father was a religious man. He went to church each Sunday, sang every hymn, and was a good example of a truly successful man. But until two tragic incidents came into my father's life several winters ago, I had never fully understood what it is to be a truly religious man. The faith he gave me was the greatest gift a father can give a son.

February is a cold month in Indiana, and last February was no exception. One school night as I studied my chemistry, I heard the fire alarm blow loudly. In a rural community like ours there is only a volunteer fire department. I hurried outside to join the others who were watching the firemen rush to the blaze. As I glanced upward, I realized that the billows of smoke filling the darkening night were coming from the direction of my father's furniture store.

Minutes later I stood beside my parents and watched one of Indiana's most fashionable furniture stores go up in flames. As hundreds of community residents rushed to save the furniture from the fire, I studied my parents' faces carefully. The yellowish light from the blaze reflected the grief in their faces. They did not shed a tear; they looked straight ahead and held their heads high.

Later that evening we returned home. The damage already had been estimated at $250,000, and the fire was still blazing. We gathered in the den and quietly thought about the evening. Finally father spoke. I had expected him to just give up. He and his brother had worked for 18 years to build an ideal furniture outlet, one that was awarded a national prize. Now that proud store was a pile of black ashes.

To my surprise, father gave thanks to God in those quiet moments. He thanked God for a wonderful family, many wonderful friends, and above all, an undying faith. I couldn't believe my ears! How could he be so thankful? How could God do such a thing to us? How would we survive?

I didn't sleep well that night. I kept thinking about my father. His whole life had been destroyed, and yet he was willing to strike out again, to rebuild his loss because of his faith! Where was mine?

The very next day father began rebuilding his dream. Along with his brother he worked long and hard each day, and there were many problems.

Finally in May, the store was reopened, more beautiful than before, all because father never gave up.

And then the second tragedy struck. We found out that father had active tuberculosis. He was immediately put to bed, isolated, and confined to his room for a period of six to eight months. I was stunned. For a while, I hated God. Then I began to notice father. He never blinked an eye when told of his illness. He went to bed and I heard him remark again how thankful he was that he had a faith to live by.

I learned a great deal that summer by watching over father. He didn't complain once. He learned Spanish as a hobby and never let us become discouraged, even when things seemed as if they could never be made right again.

As I tried to make him happy and comfortable, I began to look at myself. Could I ever have as much faith as he had? How could I develop it?

As I tried to help him, I found myself being helped. Each day a little of his belief began to take root in me. I began to realize that true faith never hides behind weak men. It is a prized possession that must be cleaned and polished regularly. It is a smile on a sick man's face, a kind word to a forgotten man, an unfailing witness to a changing world. Faith, I discovered, is life itself.

Father is much better now. The doctors are amazed at his progress and we are all awaiting the day when he can return to a normal life. He is, for me, a truly great man, and even though his tragedies have been crushing ones, the faith of each one of us has been strengthened greatly through these past months.

I have always felt that my father was a religious man. Now I know it for a fact. The faith he has shown to me will always be my most prized possession.

Susan Hayes

I Prayed to Get Caught

*T*here *was* a time when my life could have been said to be synonymous with the Latin verb *aio*—present, imperfect and having no future. If there had been a rebellious organization in my school or community at that time, I would have probably joined simply to have a cause. I wanted to stand for something, not fall for anything. But I did fall.

"Hey, what are you, a fool or something? These business dudes are cheating you blind. Anyway, they'll never miss this little stuff we swipe." That's how the whole shoplifting mess started, with a challenge and some illogical reasoning.

I started my "five-finger discount" career at the age of 11. At first, only small things were taken—candy, pencils, knickknacks. But then the dam was broken, and there was no stopping.

Why does a child shoplift? Maybe because that's the only way to get what he or she wants, or because "everyone else does it." Or maybe just to see if it can be done. My reason, if there can be one, would be the last one. I'd always mistrusted adults, and as I was stubborn and rebellious anyway, this was my chance to beat them in their world. Often I'd take something while standing right by a clerk, walk out with it, then bring it back and put it where I'd taken it from. This was a sport, and the more I won, the more I tried.

I involved my friends in my sport. We would walk into a store; they'd show me what they wanted, then we'd walk around the store. Once outside the store, they'd try to find where I put the items I took. I could slip things in their purses or pockets and they never knew it. I began taking things I didn't even want. I just couldn't walk into a store without taking something.

I knew what I was doing was wrong, but the full realization didn't dawn on me until my game had me in a deadly grip. I had been attending my church all this time. In fact, I was one of the most active youths in the church. Even though I was a church member, I thought the whole church was a big farce. I watched all those pious adults and older teens say one thing and do another. I decided I was as good as they, and if they were Christians on their way to heaven, so was I. But even then, I could sense something missing in their lives—and most of all, something was missing in mine.

By now I had been playing my game for almost four years. I now knew the penalty if I were caught and I decided it was time to stop. To my amazement, I found I couldn't stop. I couldn't control myself. This was something I couldn't handle alone.

My very best friend was a Christian of great faith. She didn't know my problem, but in her I recognized a power for which I had been searching. Her faith was so real, so relevant to her. Maybe God could become real to me, too.

I began reading my Bible, believing that the only way I would find help was through the Lord. I was desperate to break my habit, and in my desperation, I prayed. Strangely, I found myself praying to get caught.

A week later a saleslady tapped me on the shoulder and coldly said, "Take that out of your pocket, pay for it, then never come in this store again!" The Lord had answered my prayer. The game began to lose its grip. That night in February, the Lord took over my heart, mind, soul, and body.

But my trial wasn't over yet. Something said, "Go back to that store; tell that saleslady what happened to you." I couldn't do that, I just couldn't. I didn't want to do it, especially by myself. I prayed about what I should do—and suddenly I knew I could do it, for I wouldn't be alone. I knew that the Lord would be with me.

The first Saturday in April I walked into the store and said to the saleslady, Mrs. Lollis, "Ma'am, you caught me shoplifting in here about a month ago; but I want to tell you that after that, I found the Lord and by my faith in him which he gives me, I won't do it again. I'm sorry about the other time."

Tears came to her eyes, which told me her reply. With a heart happier than it had ever been, I walked out with the knowledge I was free now, totally free. Through faith, my Lord taught me to realize that a little wealth gained honestly is better than great wealth gained dishonestly, for a life of doing right is the wisest life there is.

My life is no longer like that Latin verb *aio*. I am still present and still imperfect. But now through faith I have a future—a lifetime with the Lord. That makes the greatest future of all.

Jerry Dolph Lee

The Boy Who Stood Alone

I shall never forget the feeling I had that morning four years ago when I started to school. It was an awesome hope that somehow God would help me through this day, for only the night before, I had decided to make a complete break with my old crowd—whose friendships I had enjoyed since kindergarten—in order to live by my Christian convictions.

What a poor candidate I was to stand alone! I had been a high school freshman only a few months—inarticulate, with about 20 pounds of baby fat, and a speech impediment. I seemed to be afraid to assert myself in any way, and let others take the lead.

I had lived in a happy world of church and community-centered activities. The first clouds began to gather over my sunny world when suddenly my friends seemed to start changing overnight. Everyone seemed to feel the need to do all sorts of crazy things in order to appear more grown-up to the older students.

With this trend already going in our crowd, I suppose everyone was ripe for the new boy who moved to town and subtly took over the leadership of the group. Before long, he was suggesting and leading the boys into all sorts of daring escapades which I knew were wrong. When I was reluctant to participate, they began leaving me out of things and even ridiculing me openly.

I was so disturbed I finally blurted out my inner turmoil to my older sister, a senior. Sis had always lent a listening ear to my problems and was fiercely loyal to my older brother and me, defending and championing us when we were right.

Sis was not one to remain silent. With fire in her eyes, she burst into the living room where mom and my little sister were reading. She said, "Mother, Jerry does not have one single person to go around with at school because Cal [the new boy] has turned all his friends against him just because he is trying to stay out of trouble."

Sis's statement refueled my anger toward the whole crowd, but especially Cal, and I said, "Mom, I hate that Cal Walters and if I was big enough, I would beat him up."

When mom finally spoke, she said, "Son, I know how you must feel when someone has done something like that to you—but we know that anger and hatred aren't acceptable to our Lord; so why don't we all sit down and you tell him the whole situation in your own language—and ask him to control your feelings and work the situation out?"

I guess mom could tell by the look I gave her that I didn't think the Lord would help me with anything in my present state of mind, so she repeated, "Tell him in your own words just what you told me. He will understand and then we will all ask him for his help in this problem."

She read some words from the Bible she consulted so often, and they seemed to penetrate my very soul.

Then we all prayed, as was our family custom, and I falteringly unburdened my soul to Jesus.

I felt strangely relieved and at peace that night; but the next morning going to school, I was suddenly besieged by doubts and fears. Did I really have the courage to go around by myself? To face their taunts and snubs? I remembered that God had promised to be with us in times of trouble, but though my fears were stilled, nothing helped my loneliness. I felt a sharp pain when I saw the crowd going their way without me—and seemingly having so much fun.

Since the days and months dragged along with no one to share them, I began to watch the football team work out in the afternoons. One of the coaches noticed me one day and asked if I would like to go out for the team. I couldn't imagine being out there since I was such a poor physical specimen, but he said, "Oh, come on, you might make a football player one of these days." I realize now he thought he might develop me for later years since I was a freshman. Much to my surprise, I enjoyed the team spirit and realized I would like the game if I had more stamina.

School ended and I had my first real job that summer, with long grueling hours and hard labor working with a logging operation in the woods. It had unexpected rewards, however, and my baby fat melted away quickly and my muscles grew a little stronger each day as I grew accustomed to the job. I also began to shoot upward in height; and when school opened that fall, I could hardly wait to play football.

I had met a new group of boys that I worked with that summer; and when school started, it seemed to be the natural thing for us to do things together. I scarcely noticed at first but the telephone and doorbell began to ring for me again.

A school event required inviting a date—and to my surprise the girl whom I secretly admired accepted my date invitation with apparent pleasure. As time went by, friendships developed with several girls, and a certain mixed crowd emerged at school. I experienced the warm feeling of acceptance with this group.

Somewhere along the line, I lost my speech impediment and also joined the debate team, since I was no longer afraid to speak up for my beliefs.

Time passed swiftly and in the spring of my junior year, excitement was high as school elections were being announced. I was never particularly interested in these, but as I sat in the auditorium hardly listening, I realized the principal had called my name and I sat bolt upright as he repeated, "Favorite junior boy student, elected by the junior class—Jerry Lee." I was stunned.

A few months later, as we assembled once again in the auditorium, the principal presented me with a similar award on which the entire student body had voted. I knew then beyond a doubt that only a kind and beneficent God could have brought about the fantastic events of those past three years.

But I was never deceived for a moment that God wanted me to feel any personal glory—only amazement at the things he could accomplish with the most insignificant life, if it is surrendered to him.

John Morton

The Big Race

I couldn't believe it. I had qualified for the finals of the state track meet, and this was the big day.

Ever since I was eight years old, I'd watched the summer Olympics and the NCAA championship meets, and if there was anything I wanted, it was to run in one of those events. I made up my mind that I was going to, and winning the state high school meet had to be the first step.

Four months before this meet, I had given up everything, even basketball, just to start running. I had to get in shape. Last year, when I was a sophomore, I loafed through spring practice and finished the half-mile in fifth place. My coaches were satisfied, my friends were satisfied—everybody was satisfied except me, because I knew I could have done better with more work.

Now, the coach, Mr. Cooper, and the assistant coach, Mr. Brookhart, were new, and they cared—boy, they really cared. The first day of official practice I came home sicker than a dog and I went straight to bed, despising track and everything it stood for. But when the first couple of meets came rolling by and I finished with two firsts and a second, I began to enjoy it.

I went ripping into April with the sixth fastest half-mile and the tenth best quarter-mile in the state. Then came the big meets with all of the metropolitan schools. Here is where the work really counted. In the Denver Metro Meet with 18 schools, I finished second in the half-mile.

I seemed to do better as the competition increased. The preliminaries in the state track meet were held the night before the finals, and I had the second fastest time. I seemed a sure bet to place in the finals.

Now here I was. They were calling first call for the 880-yard run over the loudspeaker. My heart seemed to jump and then stop somewhere in my throat. It felt like a boxing match was going on in my stomach. I could hardly breathe. I ran up and down beside the track a few times to see if I could loosen up—loosen up! I was getting more tense all of the time.

I wanted to pray that I would win, but that would mean that I was praying for someone else to lose, and I couldn't do that. Every boy there wanted to win as much as I did.

Last call for the 880-yard run. As I reported, they called our names over the speaker. I had a bad place, on the outside lane.

The starter said, "On your mark. . . . Get ready. . . ." The gun was up, and I jumped it. A false start. If I did it again, I would be disqualified.

The gun went off. Because I was on the outside, I was out in front. It's hard to know, when you're in this position, just how fast to go. If you start out too fast, you don't have anything left at the finish.

Those on the inside lanes were moving up on me. I let them pass. I always run near the middle until the last lap, and then I pour it on. I was still somewhere in the middle as we finished the first lap. As we rounded the third turn,

I moved to the outside to pass, and just as I did, someone caught my left foot. I began to stumble—two, three steps, and then I was lying on the track.

It seemed I was there a long time, but in reality it must only have been a moment, while I decided whether to finish the race or walk off the track. I didn't stand a chance now of coming in anywhere, but I wasn't a quitter, so I decided to finish.

The coach was waiting for me. He didn't say anything; he just put his arm around my shoulders. My elbow and knee were cut and smarting, but those cuts didn't go as deep as my disappointment.

In 17 years of life this was the worst thing that had ever happened to me. I had always believed that what often seemed a calamity would later turn out to be best. It was hard to look at it this way, especially that evening, but the more I thought about it, the more I thought, *My faith has always worked for me before, why not now?*

I opened my Bible, and God must have been guiding me, for I turned right to Psalm 37. My eye fell on verse 24, and he was speaking to me: "Though he stumble, he will not fall, for the Lord upholds him with his hand."

I felt better. It is easy to have faith when things are going right, but now I knew that God was there even when things didn't go right.

Now, a year has passed, and since I am a senior, this is the most important year. I do not know how this year's meet will go, but I know that because of my disappointment last year, I am working even harder to achieve what I missed then. Maybe that was God's plan.

Paula Hering

I Really Am Going to Change

I 've seen a lot of you kids on drugs get that religious kick, but it won't last. You'll be off of it in two weeks." There was a smirk in my teacher' voice.

"No, this is for real," I cried. "I'll prove to you it is real."

She laughed, "It's just a passing fancy with you. I'll bet you fifty cents you won't make it till the end of the school year." Her words stung me. I was hurt and I took her up on her challenge. Right then I was determined to make it.

It all started in junior high school when I started popping reds. To be in the hard crowd you had to do your thing with them. The older kids were bragging to us about being on harder stuff. Everyone of us kept going up the ladder, finding stronger things to get ripped with.

By the 10th grade my friends began to say to me, "You're hooked; you can't quit."

I always protested, "I can quit anytime I want to." One day just to prove I could, I tried and then I realized I was hooked. I couldn't stop if I wanted to. When I realized this,

I gave up and started dropping harder drugs. It was at this time my grandmother prevailed on me to go to church with her. I didn't want to, but I went.

I was sitting with some of my girlfriends. When the altar call was given, the girl beside me said, "Let's go forward." I said, "No way, get lost, I'm not going." Before I could realize what had happened, she gave me a shove out into the aisle, with her behind me pushing. It was either make a scene or keep going to the altar.

A young Christian girl came and knelt beside me. We were to become very close friends. She said, "God can help you. God can do anything."

I looked at her in disbelief. "Don't put me on. You mean God can help me get off heavy stuff?"

"Yes," she replied, "God can help you." She seemed to believe what she had said.

"Okay, I'll try it," I replied. She prayed and I prayed with her. From that moment I kicked the dope habit.

It was when I told my teacher at school my experience of the night before that she became skeptical and laughed at me. And she was the one person I had felt would be understanding and encouraging. As I walked down the hall I was hurt and angry. I could have cried. At that moment I was determined more than anything else in the world to prove she was wrong.

A short time later in one of her classes my arm went completely numb, and my vision became blurred. I couldn't think. My body ached with pain. The teacher came over to me. "What's the matter with you?"

"I can't see," I replied.

"Are you taking dope?" she asked.

"No, I told you I had quit completely."

She looked panicky. "You can't just suddenly stop!" She helped me to a cot to lie down until the numbness and dizziness went away.

The next day the teacher called me aside. "Any time one of these flashbacks hits you, come to me," she said. "If you happen to be in another class and they ask you why you are leaving, tell them I requested you to do some work for me. I will write you a pass, and you can go lie down until you snap out of it."

Suddenly I felt warm and happy all over. My teacher wasn't against me. She wanted to help. It was then I realized she had said what she had to give me a determination to kick the habit. I had a friend.

In the weeks that followed, time after time, I went to her when the flashbacks would hit me. Very few words were spoken. It was as if she were afraid she might break the spell. But if time permitted, she would sit and visit with me about other things in general. In her own way there were words of encouragement, like, "You've really changed, I can tell a difference," or, "You're really looking good today."

What I noticed more than anything else was the way she looked at me. It wasn't with that "You poor thing; I feel sorry for you" look any longer. I could see concern in her eyes. As the days passed, it turned to a look of hope and then to a pleased look. This was followed by a happy look. Then later there was a proud look in her eyes when she looked at me.

At times I felt completely free. In these moments I was truly happy, which I had never been before.

When I told the crowd I hung out with I had kicked the habit and was going to church, they roared with laughter. Their laughter soon turned to ridicule. As time passed and they saw I was really serious, they dropped me. However, by this time I had many new friends in the church.

This is a life I thought would be dull and that I would hate. I must admit I was surprised—I really enjoyed my new way of life. I came in contact with new young people who had goals and a completely different concept of life. I liked it. Life became more than just existing. There were beautiful things to be done to help others.

The battle raged through the winter of my tenth-grade year but by spring I was free of any more flashbacks. I had won the hardest battle of my life.

Then it was the end of the school year and time for the presenting of grades and special awards to outstanding students. I couldn't believe it when I was called forward for an award. At what could I have possibly excelled? I could hardly wait to read the certificate that was handed to me. It read: Certificate of Award, to Paula Hering, Who Has Found the Key to Life. Glued to the bottom was 50 cents. My teacher was saying in her way, "I'm proud of you, Paula. You won."

Merry Hirt

The Invitation

ike many other Christian youth, I began my religious instruction at an early age. It was the usual Sunday school routine where all the preschool kids sing songs and act out finger plays to better help them understand Jesus. This sounded very nice to my young ears—God was some type of good-natured old grandfather who sat upon a throne in heaven and watched over us to make sure that we behaved.

As the years went by and I finished my church instruction, I became confused and felt that I could take or leave God. I thought that I would have more time for religion when I got older and had nothing better to do. I wanted to live while I was young—I decided I was not going to be tied down by a God who made all sorts of outrageous demands!

In my late teen years I began to get very interested in the opposite sex. When I was 17 I fell in love with a very special boy at my high school. This was not puppy love or my first love or anything like that—I was positive that this was the guy for me. I had never met anyone like him before.

We went everywhere together and were sure that in time we would be married. My whole world revolved around him. Occasionally we would have fights and for both of us these fights took us through a personal agony. Eventually we made up and our love would be deeper than ever.

As time passed we began to talk more seriously about how it would be when we were married. We also started discussing sex and the role that it would play in our married life.

Meanwhile we necked and petted. After a while things became a little heated at times but we were not worried. There was no reason to be. After all, we were mature young adults who were intelligent enough to know how to handle ourselves.

Then one evening after the wedding of one of his closest friends, we went over to my boyfriend's house. His parents were not home and he began to talk of how nice it would be if it was our house and we had been the ones getting married. I knew what he meant and I began to feel uneasy.

He wanted to show me his bedroom and I convinced myself that there was no harm in just taking a little look. He would never take advantage of me; he loved me too much. After we were inside his bedroom, I turned to him and when I saw the look in his eyes, I knew that we were playing with fire. My emotions were mixed and my hands were trembling. I knew he felt the same way. Many thoughts flashed through my mind: Why not? We'll never get caught. No one will ever have to know. We love each other and should have the right to express it. After all, we're going to be married someday.

And then God really came into my life. For I suddenly saw that the sex act was his gift to us as a part of the holy institution of marriage. I had no right to steal something that did not belong to me. I had no right to misuse one of God's gifts.

At the same time I knew somehow that God would never condemn me for what we were thinking of doing and that made the love of God flow through me even more. My parents were always close to me and now I understood the reason for their happiness together. They had such a strong relationship with God that nothing could upset them for long.

I looked earnestly at my boyfriend and tried to express to him my feelings. I could not seem to find the right words. We watched each other for a moment and then he said, "Pray for us."

I did and thanked God for showing us his way—for giving us the strength to say no when we had none of our own.

Glenda Jones

The Day My Faith Meant the Most to Me

One afternoon in December, my little sister and I bounded off the school bus and into our house. Tonight would surely be different—tonight mom would greet us with that special exuberant spirit all her own. The Christmas spirit was just too infectious, especially for mom, who usually was the most susceptible one of all. Into the kitchen we trounced, bubbling over with joy. But the bubbles soon burst as we stared at the lone piece of paper lying on the table. My happy little world ended as I read dad's familiar scrawl.

All we could see were those dreaded words looming before our eyes. "I have taken mother to Cherokee—Dad." Cherokee was an accepted joke around our school. Seldom did a day go by when someone didn't make some smart remark about a certain person being bound for a straitjacket at Cherokee. How I had howled at such humor then!

Never could I feel the same way again. It was as if a door of my life had slammed shut, denying me my former carefree days. Oh, I had known that mom had not been alert for several months, but I had refused to face the situation. Now I had no choice but to accept the fact that mom—my own mother—was mentally ill and might not be home for months!

And who did that leave in charge as "chief cook and bottle washer?" Me—15-year-old me. Dazedly, I threw together a few meager scraps which hardly could be considered a meal. I was too stunned to care about anything except. . . what was I going to do? How could I manage a household and keep my grades up at the same time? Would I have to sacrifice my social life?

The back door slammed and my dad came in. Time can erase every other memory, but I can never forget his face at that moment—eyes so devoid of emotion and hope as to seem transparent, his whole face frozen in an expression of despair. One look and I knew that my problems were insignificant compared with those my dad had to shoulder.

Right then and there I made up my mind that, no matter what, our family would hold the fort for dad's sake. Although I knew I could never replace mom (and didn't intend to try), I would do my own best to make things easier for my family.

I could end the story right here by saying that turning to God in my hour of despair gave me the needed strength and confidence. But God was the farthest from my thoughts during that next week. "After all," I reasoned bitterly, "if God let such misfortune happen to a family who didn't deserve it, then surely my prayers—if even heard—would be unwelcome and go unanswered."

As if matters weren't already bad enough, gradually I began to feel sorry for myself—for the bad stroke of fate, for the additional responsibility and work. My temper became short. I would lash out at my little sister for leaving her dirty socks on the davenport. I would argue with dad as though it were I who ran everything in the household. I couldn't understand the puzzled and hurt replies I received.

Finally December 24 arrived. But this year it was more than just Christmas Eve; it was the day at last that dad and I could visit mom. That morning, my bitter ways seemed sweetened somewhat by the magical effect of the day and I began to think of someone beside myself. I began to realize what a lonely Christmas mom and many others like her would be spending. By the time we were ready to leave, I was loaded down with presents—not only for mom, but paper plates of candy and cookies my sister and I had made for others at Cherokee.

Since my dad had an appointment with mom's doctor before we could visit her, I waited in the lobby. While sitting in the great hallway filled with other visitors and with patients going home for the holidays, my old resentment began to tug at my conscience. Once again I began to wonder how God could be so merciless as to let such an illness strike us.

"You look very sad," said a voice that snapped me back to reality. "That's no way to be on Christmas Eve." It was the elderly lady sitting next to me. In no time I was deep in conversation with her.

My new friend was of such a sunny nature that it came as a surprise for me to learn that her son was a patient in Cherokee. Later I learned that her daughter at home was paralyzed by polio from the waist down. Accepting her handicap, this girl had made the most of her abilities and was currently writing a novel. It seems impossible that with all the heartache she had suffered, this woman could be so cheerful and optimistic, so outgoing. Before I even realized it—I heard myself pouring out all my problems just as if she were an old friend.

When I had finished, she grew very serious and carefully explained to me how one simple act—prayer—had relieved her of an unaccountable amount of grief and had made her reliance upon God strong and vital. So at last was unlocked the mystery of this woman's cheerful perseverance. She soon made me realize that my prayers would have to be from the heart and not of a superficial type. When she had prayed for her children, she had asked God "to take care of them as he saw fit, not as I saw." In such a manner, must I ask God for help. For only then would I feel that my burden had been lightened. At last I realized that I had been shunning the only One who could help me but, nevertheless, he had been waiting patiently by my side until I could "see the light" and put my wholehearted trust in him.

Maybe it was God watching over me who sent such a person to teach me one of the most important lessons of life. I'd rather believe that it was also the magic of Christmas Eve and the fact that on such a day, many years ago, the greatest miracle of all humankind took place, a miracle that made possible such minor miracles as had taken place this particular day.

Yes, the day my faith meant the most to me was the day I found it on a snowy Christmas Eve in the lobby of a mental hospital. There I found faith that sustained me over the year that my mother struggled up the rocky road to recovery.

Brian Rexroad

How to Handle
a Broken Dream

On a day in mid-August, I awoke to a beautiful sunny morning. That day was to be the beginning of a long-awaited dream for me. I was 15 years old and dedicated to sports. I had been captain of my junior high school football and basketball teams and catcher on the baseball team; I was an avid snow skier. I knew one day I would be a professional athlete, and I hoped it would be as a basketball player. I worked hard and practiced diligently toward my career goal. It was not the idea of personal stardom I glorified in, but the excitement of competition with other people and with myself to do better.

That day I was to attend the first official football conditioning practice of the year at Cuyahoga Falls High School. I felt confident and eager as I went on the field at nine that morning.

Six-foot-one and weighing 193 pounds, I was a defensive tackle and as part of my conditioning, that morning I tackled a Hooker-tack-matic machine, a training aid for football players, that was set for its maximum of 300 pounds of pressure. Upon my contact with the dummy, the machine jammed in its track. Instantly I dropped to the ground unable to move. Paralyzed, I lay on the field for 45 minutes. During that agonizing time the trainer pulled my helmet off my head and then rubbed a pencil over the nerve areas of my body. I felt nothing. Scared? You bet I was.

A bit later, however, feeling returned from my waist down and I managed to get on my feet. The trainer helped me to his car and drove me to a hospital. There he told them he thought I had a pinched nerve. But the X-rays showed that my neck was broken.

That was the beginning of a frightening nightmare for me.

The doctors told me and my family that my days as a football player were over. I was put in neck traction for 40 days. My head was immobilized with weights to keep me from turning. The nerves in my hands and arms were damaged. Though they hurt, I slowly regained use of them.

During those next 40 days I had a lot of time to think. Fear and depression seized me, but each time I felt really discouraged, something would happen to lift my spirits.

Coaches from other schools wrote me letters of encouragement. College coaches sent me information on their athletic programs, saying they were interested in me as a basketball player. That was medicine I needed. Ministers of many faiths visited with me and prayed for me, along with friends and relatives.

Then a wonderful man came to see me. I had never met him before, and I will never forget the look in his eyes as he told me that I was a miracle, that it was amazing that I was alive. That man was Coach Joe Pisani, the director of the Fellowship of Christian Athletes at my school. He never coached me on a football field, but he has and still is coaching me on God's field.

The days passed and my body grew thinner, but my faith grew thicker. Finally the day came for me to be put into a minerva-jacket body cast—a 30-pound cast that started at my hips and extended up over my head. Only my arms and face were exposed. At first I felt like I was being smothered in the trunk of a tree.

Slowly my therapist taught me to walk again. What a great feeling it was to get off my back and onto my feet, even though they didn't work just right at first. The little kids in the hospital called me The Lurch or The Mummy. Their cries of pain or discomfort turned into laughter when they saw me walking in the hallway.

Finally the day to go home arrived. It was a homecoming of welcome signs, happy tears, and greetings from many friends. The days that followed made me feel one day closer to returning to a normal life and basketball.

After four weeks at home, my cast was removed. I then wore a steel neck brace 24 hours a day for six weeks. When that time was finally up, we made our trip to the doctor to have the brace removed so I could start life free again. That was the day we had anxiously awaited.

But the X-rays showed that my neck had not healed correctly. I must have a neck fusion or my head would hang on my chest. We must start all over again. Painfully I accepted this latest blow.

Then came the biggest blow of all. The doctor told me I could never return to any contact sports again. A direct blow to the top of my head would be fatal to me. There went my dreams of something I wanted more than anything else—a career as a professional basketball player.

That was the day my life fell apart. I didn't think there was anything left for me in life. *Why me? Why me?* I thought. My heart hurt so much I will never be able to describe it. *Why? Why?* I kept wondering.

Yet after a few hours of depression, something inside me said, "Don't give up. Keep fighting." So I did, knowing that God would somehow take care of me. I prayed for the strength to endure, to handle whatever lay in store.

In January of the next year, I had a six-hour operation. Bone was removed from my hip and fused into my neck. Six wires were wrapped about my neck vertebrae. Those wires will be my lifelong companions, but my operation was a masterpiece of surgery. The pain that followed became a sport for me, something for me to conquer—if I fought hard enough.

Once again I was put into the neck brace, which I then wore for six months. Finally, once again, it was time for my checkup. Great news this time. Off came the brace; the X-rays looked good. My prayers had been answered.

Even though I long for the competition and exhilaration of the basketball court, I realize now just how lucky I am. I can stand on my own two feet and at least shoot baskets with my own hands and arms. My paralysis is gone, my nerves are healed and even though my neck is partially stiff, I'm alive.

I'll always remember my mother saying while I was in the hospital, "The doctors will care for Brian now, but God cared for him while he was lying on that field." Now I know what she said was true.

I know now that while I may never need a basketball coach again, I have found a Coach who will always be there to guide me. He has coached me back to a world of faith, love, and life. And with him there rooting for me, I know I can find a career that's right for me and enjoy it as much as I once loved playing sports. Only my Coach knows why the accident happened and what lies ahead as a result. Whatever it is, I know it will be the best thing for me. He's brought me a long way already.

Marjorie Garrison

Night of Fear

I don't really know why I decided to walk those three miles to my friend's house that night. I think I wanted so badly to be a cheerleader and gain the popularity which would come with it. Well, I hadn't made it and I felt pretty disgusted with myself. Walking would help ease my pent-up feelings.

I really thought I allowed myself enough time to get there before it got dark but by the time I reached the high school, about two miles from my home, the street lights were coming on and twilight was setting in. I hastened my steps and continued on.

I remembered telling my friend to come and meet me with her car if I hadn't reached her home in an hour or so. So, I concluded, I had to walk along the route that she normally took to come to my house. That route led me through a wooded area. There were homes on only one side of the street and that is where I walked.

My mind was filled with thoughts of the past day and I didn't think much about the man standing with his back to me about three feet from the path I was following. Soon I heard footsteps and I assumed that he was walking his dog. Night had fallen by this time; the only light was that of headlights from passing cars or an occasional street light.

I walked on, still deep in thought though the train of it had changed. I remember thinking of the Lord and how he had promised to always be with his children and keep them safe. I began to walk faster but the only thing that accomplished was clumsiness. I tripped over a small wire fence and sprawled headlong onto the ground. I jumped to my feet and a man's voice asked if I was all right. He then walked by and appeared to turn a corner, loosening his tie as he went.

At that instant there was a lull in traffic. Suddenly the same man came up behind me, quickly encircled my neck with his tie and covered my mouth with his hand. He forced me back into the woods as I struggled and prayed for a car to come toward us to illuminate the scene.

He pushed me to the ground and knelt beside me, pinning me down. Pulling a knife from his pocket, he said, "Don't scream or I'll kill you." I struggled violently and began to pray aloud over and over: "Oh, Jesus! Help me! Help me!" The man struck me on the sides of my head, trying to silence me. I begged him to let me go and kept calling on the Lord to help me.

Suddenly he stopped. In a calmer voice he said, "Okay, I'll let you go. But just walk with me for a while first." Then the Lord filled me with a calm and assurance that I had never known before. I got to my feet and we began to walk through the woods. At first he kept the tie around my neck and made me walk ahead. But after awhile, when I told him I wouldn't run away if he would promise to let me go later, he removed the tie.

As we walked, we talked. The first thing he said was a remark about my prayers and my calm attitude. "My Lord is with me and is helping me," I explained. I don't think he quite understood my words, but I believe he felt the Lord's presence there. He actually began to help me over rough places in the ground and even expressed concern for my safety.

I figured out later that we must have talked for about an hour and a half. The man told me some things about his troubled past and I told him God could help him with all of his problems, no matter what they were.

When he released me the man asked me to forgive him and then told me to run to the first house and call my parents. He said he didn't want anything to happen to me. I knew a friend who lived in the area and I ran there faster than I've ever run before.

All I can say now is that I believe God still performs miracles and I pray that he will work in the life of that man who so desperately needs him.

Shirley Tatro

The Moment

ithout really meaning to, I had fallen into a beautiful and innocent young love. For the first time in my life I began to give of myself unselfishly. And the boy I had come to love returned twofold any happiness that I may have given him. I guess that is the wonderful thing about true affection.

Through our moments together, our relationship continued to grow into one of deep understanding and mutual respect and trust. Each day that I wore his ring on my finger only added to the love I felt in my heart.

But a feeling of such complete devotion has a funny way of playing tricks on a person. And when you are only 17, a year becomes a long time to have been telling a guy, "I love you." So as we shared these deep feelings for each other we explored the thrills of kisses and caresses together.

I think we always knew that a moment of final decision was inevitable. Yet we pushed such serious thoughts to the back of our minds, telling ourselves, "It won't happen this time."

But tomorrow always arrives, and our time also came. After months of nights filled with dark roads and searching kisses, we encountered a brick wall that had only one door. We now had a choice to make. It would be so easy to go through that door, with the excuse, "We're doing it out of love." Yet we knew we would pay a very dear price—our innocence.

Maybe the complete unselfishness that I had thought we felt was not so complete after all, for on that night there was something in each of us that made us stop. Or perhaps we both knew we would be losing something that could never be replaced, and we just could not bring ourselves to make that sacrifice. Whatever the reason, we didn't open that door that night. But we had at last realized that we could be terribly tempted—and we knew that many nights and temptations lay before us.

We had to find some way either to change or justify the thing we were doing. We became aware of one fact— our awful misconception that love and sex are synonymous was on the verge of destroying us. We had begun to forget how to laugh and be happy just that we were together. Tears no longer eased the shame. Words became hollow and mean-ingless sounds. We needed a solution, but where could we turn?

It is a little ironic that the answer to our question was so simple and was there with us all the time. It came, along with one of the greatest moments in my relationship with the boy I love, when he held me and said, "Let's pray." Only two small words, but they lifted the burden from our shoul-ders and put it in the hands of someone far, far stronger. The God that had given us these bodies, these emotions, and these desires would now guide us in their use.

We found that the road back is not an easy one. Some-times we stumble and fall, but there is always a firm and gentle hand to pick us up and urge us on our way.

We know now that a small part of us died that night, but at the same time a new seed of faith was planted and began to grow.

Perhaps someday, if it is his will, the God who gave us the courage to turn back and keep that beautiful love we held will give us his blessings to return to that door, open it, and really begin our lives together.

Until that day, my guy and I have an obligation to keep. We have promised to care for and nourish our young love until one day when it blooms in full glory.

Karen Holmes

Room 18

*H*ot and sticky—that's how I felt, but it didn't matter because I was with Mike. All that seemed to matter to us was making each other happy, so Mike and I had decided to go on a picnic at Lansbrook Park, something we had never done before.

After a quick lunch of fried chicken and coleslaw, we climbed the ivy-covered rock steps that lead to the tennis courts. Mike drew the leaves aside, brushed the dirt from the top step and sat down. Motioning me to sit beside him, he asked me what I wanted to do that night.

"I don't care. What do you want to do?"

"I want to get a motel room," he answered.

I looked up at him in astonishment. "You're joking," I said unbelievingly.

"No," he said, "I'm serious."

"What will I tell my mom?"

"Tell her we're going to a baseball game and out to eat," Mike said. "I'll have you home by midnight."

I still wasn't sure he was serious. We had voiced our opinions on premarital sex and I had said I thought it was strictly a question of one's own morals. But I hadn't said how I felt about it.

"What time will you pick me up?" I asked.

"Oh, I don't know," Mike said, "probably around 6:30."

"OK, I'll be ready at 6:30 and not a minute earlier," I said, "but you better take me home now, so I can have time to get ready." He looked at me, smiled and kissed me on my forehead, something he does when I need reassuring.

Then he jumped up, grabbed the picnic basket and my arm and said, "I'll race you to the car." I wasted no time, but went sprinting down the steps. I could feel Mike close at my heels. We went running through the open field, the sun playing tricks with our eyes, and our hearts beating faster and faster.

During the short trip to my house, we were silent. As I walked slowly toward my front door, thinking about the plans we had made, I thought, *What's wrong with me?* I had somehow known that my relationship with Mike would eventually lead to more and more intimacy. Now I knew I should have started saying no to a lot of things a long time ago.

My mother was sitting at the kitchen table sewing. I pretended to look through the mail on the desk, then said, "Mike and I are going to a baseball game and then to dinner tonight."

"OK," she said. "Oh, by the way, you received a letter from your Sunday school class; I put it on your desk."

I went to my room and closed the door. I found the letter lying on my desk, but I didn't need to read it. They always said the same thing: "Dear Karen, we miss you and hope you will be with us this Sunday. Your Sunday school class." I wondered what my Sunday school class would think if they knew where I was going at 6:30.

I glanced at the clock. I had only an hour to get ready and I needed time to think. I locked myself in the bathroom and ran bath water.

As I lay back in the hot water, I thought, *What am I getting so uptight about? People do it all the time. Why should Mike and I be any different? Besides, I owe it to him.* Then I started thinking about the ease with which Mike had said, "I want to get a motel room." Tonight was going to be an entirely different experience for him than for me. He wasn't losing anything. I was.

After brushing my hair and applying fresh make-up, I had about one second to continue with my thinking. Mike was right on time.

Again in the car there was silence. What could I say to him? Couldn't he tell by my actions I didn't want to go to some cheap motel room?

Nothing was said until Mike spoke. "It's all ours, room eighteen." My stomach fell. Mike opened my door for me as he groped in his pocket for the key to the room. "I got the room before I picked you up," he announced.

I walked inside while Mike struggled to get the key back out of the lock. I turned around only to come face to face with him. He put his arms around me and held me. I was so scared. I had to tell him how I felt, but I didn't know how.

Suddenly I found myself praying, asking God to help me. I began to feel warm, as I had that afternoon when running in the sun. For the first time in my life, I felt the presence of God. I looked up at Mike. He had a curious expression on his face. "Mike," I said, "can we talk?"

"Sure," he replied. I wondered if he already knew what I was about to say.

"Mike, I'm not ready," I said, looking down at my toes.

He lifted my chin, kissed me lightly on the forehead and said, "Karen, all you had to do was tell me. I don't want you to do anything you feel is wrong."

Never before had Mike been so kind and understanding. And then I thought, *Never before have I let God help me with a problem. I've always tried to shut him out and do it all on my own.*

That night opened my eyes to a faith I had never known, a faith that lets me know God is always near when I need him. All I had to do was open my heart and let him come in.

Anne Shelly

The Accident

Lying on the asphalt of the runway at the Van Nuys Airport, I clutched my bleeding left side with my right hand. I was in great pain. My boyfriend stood beside me, screaming. I turned to comfort him and saw my left arm. It was lying a foot from my body.

My arm had been completely severed by the propeller of a small Cessna airplane. I reached out to touch it. I wanted a whole and complete body. Then I grew angry. The idea of having only one arm repulsed me. I was 15. I love to swim, to dance. Silently I shouted, "No!" Death, so very close, was a welcome thought.

The sound of my boyfriend's voice swept me away from the thought of death. Remembering my faith, I asked God for my arm back.

I have had faith in God since I was very young. When I was 11, my family finally settled into a church. We felt welcomed and comfortable for the first time. Love and support surrounded us. We attended classes which reaffirmed our trust in God.

As I learned and grew, I began to use my faith. I had

my prayers answered with little things—good grades on tests in school, harmony instead of meaningless spats with my brothers. With each passing manifestation of belief, I became more aware of the importance of faith; I trusted God.

There on the airport runway, my arm separated from my body, I turned to God. Pain left. Calmness soothed my body. God was with me. Not as a prayer, or some hopeful wish, but through his presence, holding me in protective arms.

The fire rescue squad arrived minutes later. While one man clamped my arteries and veins, another packed my arm in an ice-filled plastic sack. I was then rushed to Van Nuys Receiving Hospital.

The hospital called my father. (My mother was vacationing in the mountains with my youngest brother.) When he came to see me in the emergency room, I asked him to call my Sunday school teacher and have her start a circle of prayer for me and my family.

At first the doctors were going to keep me at the emergency hospital and merely sew up my armless shoulder. But one of the doctors remembered that Orthopedic Hospital in downtown Los Angeles had reimplanted a fireman's severed arm several years before. They decided to send me there. I was loaded into another ambulance and driven 20 miles over the freeways.

I felt very sleepy in the ambulance. Wanting to stay awake, I asked the attendant to whistle. The continuous rolling movement of the ambulance and the soft whistle of the attendant comforted me. I quietly began to sing "Let There Be Peace on Earth," a song we often sing at my church that has always given me a sense of God's peace.

Although it was now about ten o'clock on a summer night, the exact team of surgeons who had performed the other rare operation was available when I arrived. Three and a half hours after I had lost my arm, I went into surgery to get it back. By now the circle of prayer for me was spreading throughout the city.

After six hours of surgery, I was told that the operation might not work. The doctors explained that my body might reject the arm and that there was a danger of infection since my arm had been carried in an unsterilized plastic sack.

I did not feel concerned about the outcome. My faith told me that "in all things God works for the good of those who love him" (Rom. 8:28), and I did love God. His presence stayed with me and I had no doubt.

Ten days after the accident, I celebrated my 16th birthday. The party was held in the recreation room at the hospital. My most beloved friends were there. The newspapers and television reported on the girl who got her arm back as a birthday present and I received thousands of birthday wishes from all over the world. The light of God touched us all.

Five weeks later, with no rejection or infection, I was ready to go home. But now I was told that I would not be able to use my arm for two years. Again I trusted God to help.

On Thanksgiving Day, only four months later, I could move my fingers. Now, a year later, I can swim 40 laps, knit, sew, throw a ball, skip rope, drive, dance, participate in gym activities and hug my family and friends.

That night at the airport I trusted God with my life and my arm. Today I have both. My faith was not only reinforced that wonderful night, but the fact of God's presence became my greatest joy.

David Parsons

How to Handle a Lousy Job

*L*ife had suddenly gone sour on me. I was almost 18 years old and had nothing to look forward to. My senior year at Edsel Ford High School, which had just started, should have been a time of excitement. Instead, I was filled with the dread certainty that I would not graduate with my class. I lacked the necessary credits and had only myself to blame.

Naturally that realization didn't remove the sting of disappointment. It only made my part-time job at the gas station seem less bearable. If I had graduation to look forward to—if only I knew I could enroll in a college next fall. . . . Now I had to go to night school (which I hated the thought of) and continue to work at the station (which I hated the thought of even more).

My job helped me financially, but it sure wasn't helping me to like people. Let's face it, you don't see people at their best when you're a gas pump jockey. People are always in a hurry, blowing their horns, and yelling out orders.

You get these guys who drive up in a Lincoln Continental or a Cadillac and order two dollars' worth of gas on a credit charge. Or there's the dude who comes in during a driving rainstorm, and you stand dripping wet by his window (which he barely rolls down so he doesn't get wet) and try to understand his garbled speech while he barks out orders through a fat cigar.

Or the young drunks who flock in around 2 A.M. with their old junk cars—so misshapen they defy description. All they want is 50 cents' worth of gas and they have to take up a hurried collection for that! Or the housewife in for a grease job, completely oblivious to the fact that her kids are running rampant through the station—so you hurry to get her car serviced before they tear up the place.

Yes, I hated the thought of night school; but, heck, I had to graduate or I might end up pumping gas for the rest of my life and putting up with all these crazy people. I shuddered at the thought, jerking the nozzle carelessly out of the car's gas well. "Hey, buddy, watch the paint job, will ya!" The guy jutted his head through the open window as he yelled at me, and I had the greatest urge to grab him and yank him the rest of the way.

All my evenings were filled with similar hateful thoughts. At the end of each evening I would go home spent and depressed. I had decided that I really didn't like people and, even worse, I didn't like myself!

What had happened to me? Why had I changed? I tried to think things through as I lay sleeplessly in bed. I hadn't prayed for a long time. God, like my schoolwork, had been sloughed off—forgotten—for better things. "Oh, God," I prayed in earnest, "I need your help. I want to change. Help me to like myself—and people—again."

God has funny ways of helping people. Sometimes it's all done so subtly we don't recognize that it's his providence.

"Dave—Dave Parsons!" The fellow in the car looked familiar, but I couldn't place him. "Bob Stone," he said with a warm smile.

"Gosh, Bob, I didn't recognize you. How're things going?" I didn't have to ask that. I knew how things must be going for Bob. We had gone to high school together but Bob had become all fouled up on drugs. He was expelled from school and had barely survived death from an overdose.

Yet as we talked now, somehow I knew that this down-and-out character understood my problem. I found myself telling him the whole bit—all my complaints, my frustrations, my fears.

Was I ever in for a shock! "I guess you would still call me a freak," he said with a broad grin. "But now I'm a Jesus freak. I'm what I call an ambassador of God."

He went on to explain that when he had nearly died, he had prayed to God that if he would spare him, he'd spend the rest of his days making up for the tragic mess he had made of his life. So now he was helping other kids kick drugs.

I mentally compared myself to Bob Stone. Bob had lived through some hard knocks, but instead of going around with a chip on his shoulder and feeling sorry for himself as I had in the past, he had reached out to others and given of himself. He had turned his defeats into victories with the help of God. He had found the one thing that makes life worthwhile—a purpose in being through Jesus Christ.

It was that very night that I made my commitment to Jesus Christ. From now on, I vowed, I was going to live like a Christian—not just practice verbal religion—and try to be an example to others of what Christ can do with us.

What a wonderful opportunity I had on my job to be an ambassador of God. Think of all the people I came in contact with!

Needless to say, I didn't change right away. But those words of Bob's, "ambassador of God," stuck with me. Without realizing it, I was becoming a different person. My faith in myself and my attitude toward people improved day by day. I became enthusiastic about my job and began to whistle and laugh more.

I talked to the customers. They loved it! But, more important, I began to see people as just that—people. People with the same doubts, fears, and frustrations as I had; people with the same need for love and understanding.

The fellows with their flashy cars, too busy to be nice, were to be pitied. The housewife hadn't meant to be irresponsible. She was probably a loving wife and mother who appreciated the few moments of adult conversation. The young drunks were kids like myself—searching for a meaning in life.

Once in a while I bump into a person now who snaps at me, "What are you so cheerful about?" And I say to them, "I've got a lot going for me, thanks to God. And to me life is just wonderful."

Some go away frowning—but then there are all those who leave the pumps smiling. It's so good to help people smile!

Joel William Franks

My Victory
Over Hate

One day when I was still quite small, I got very angry at my older brother, Jim, and barked, "I hate you!" My grandpa, who overheard the display of temper, reprimanded me—nobody could make me feel two inches tall any faster than grandpa—quoting 1 John 3:15: "Anyone who hates his brother is a murderer, and you know that no murderer has eternal life in him."

But I thought, *What a ridiculous verse—I couldn't kill Jimmie. I love him. I couldn't murder anyone, especially Jim.*

From the earliest time I can remember, I have admired my brother. Everything he does, he does well—especially in sports. When he was a freshman in high school, his basketball team won the Arkansas state championship, and he was voted the most valuable player. What Jim did I wanted to do. For the three years I played on the Cotter Junior High basketball team, I played every game with this thought in mind: When I was a freshman, we would win the state championship, and I would have all of the glory that my older brother had received.

As my freshman year wore on, it became evident that we had good chances to win state. With each game, the pressure grew. Our school was old and small and faced consolidation. We just could not afford to lose—for if we lost, people might want to dissolve forever our precious Cotter High School.

We advanced to the finals of the district tournament. We were pitted against nearby Norfork, and the all-important game was being played in their home gym. All along the sidelines I thought I could see hatred in the eyes of the hometown crowd, simply because we were playing so hard to win. These same people were my friends and neighbors only yesterday. My mind slowly turned to the Bible verse Grandpa had quoted me years before. At that moment, it was easy for me to think these people had murder in their hearts for my teammates and me. So I asked God to never let me be filled with hatred toward any person.

Somehow we managed to win the game by two points and advance to the state tournament at Hampton, over 200 miles away. And as they often are in Arkansas during the last week in February, the roads were covered with ice and snow, and every mile of the way we wondered what was keeping us from ending up at the foot of some mountain. Once the coach wanted to turn back; some of the boys laughingly remarked they wished Norfork had won instead of us; but icy roads weren't going to stop us. We were on our way to win the state tournament.

After traveling that far, we seemed to press even harder to win. The first two games, both cliff-hangers, were won by the Cotter Warriors. We gave our all, straining every muscle and nerve to defeat the other team, who tried just as hard to beat us. In the second game my tensions were compounded—I fouled out and was forced to watch the last minute of play from the bench.

In the semifinals we were pitted against Ouachita County—a tall, talented all-black team of junior high boys. They were the best, and if only, if only we could beat them the final game would be easy.

The game started. We matched them basket for basket. At half time the score was tied. Victory was close, we knew, so very, very close. Then came the final tense seconds, and suddenly my beautiful dream died. We were defeated by one point. The big balloon on which I was riding—blown tight by three close games in three days, the "hairy" trip down, the nightmare victory at Norfork—had suddenly been pricked. I was deflated, defeated, empty.

My disappointment was so great that I could feel my heart surging with hatred. How easy it was at that moment to hate those black faces—shiny with sweat and excitement after a hard-fought game. And theirs was a victory that was almost ours.

How easily I could have hated the referees for a foul not called, a walking infraction not seen, a tie ball not jumped. One call reversed could have meant the difference.

Then just as these feelings of hate welled up in me, I remembered my grandpa's words, "Whosoever hateth his brother is a murderer." No, I didn't hate the black faces, I didn't hate the long black arms and legs that had won the game. I didn't hate them, the referees or anybody. I'm not a murderer. They are my brothers.

The brief moment of bitterness passed. I reached out my hand to the referee nearest me. "You called a nice game," I said.

If I live to be 100 years old, I'll never forget the look of surprise on the referee's face.

Somehow that remark was just enough to ignite my teammates, and all of us began to shake the hands, and embrace the happy boys who had just beaten us. It became a contagion of joy, real joy, and everyone was affected by it.

The very next night, Ouachita County won the Class B Junior Boys Basketball Championship, the first all-black team to win a state championship in Arkansas. We were thrilled for them. And, as it turned out, our Cotter Warriors were chosen by the coaches and officials for the highly coveted Sportsmanship Trophy.

One week later, my brother Jimmie and the senior Cotter Warriors were defeated in the semifinals of their state tournament, but they, too, won the Sportsmanship Award. We like to think that these trophies, which honor not only the coach and the players, but also the school, the community, the homes, and the churches of the school district, turned the tide against consolidation of our school.

I still attend Cotter High School. Now I'm playing on the senior basketball team. Whatever the future holds, whether we win or lose, I will never forget the night I won the greatest victory of all—the victory over hate.

Teacher, I Forgive You . . .

My friend Kerri Lynn was 15 and a lithe, bouncing freshman at South High when it happened. She had been a cheerleader in eighth grade, and really looked forward to joining South's sophomore squad. Dancing through life with tears, smiles, or a crazy philosophical streak that made one sympathize with her like a little hurt puppy, she had friends everyplace.

Then one afternoon in March, bending over to pick up a book along a four-lane highway, Kerri was hit by a car. She sprawled on the road, as her friend Jenny watched in shocked disbelief.

That March turned black.

Lapsing into a coma, Kerri lived for two weeks while nobody could do anything except look on in anguished uncertainty and pray. South High was suspended by apprehension and bewilderment that hushed conversation. Everyone kept hoping for Kerri's life until the pressure of maintaining faith was unbearable. I watched Sharyn,

Kerri's friend, believe and believe and believe, until the price she paid was a constant headache that pounded out the minutes and the hours.

And then Kerri died.

I got out of bed. After that morning I couldn't cry. I could only be increasingly bitter against the woman who had killed Kerri. Everything in me rebelled against this thinking, but I refused to listen. So I hid it under a cover of faith and illusion and tried to help those around me.

Once, at the wake, Kerri's mother held fast to my hand as she whispered, "Thank you for your braveness and words of hope, Carolyn." But it wasn't bravery, rather belief that this was a part of a friendship, helping others the way Kerri would have helped me. But this friendship and my faith also demanded that I say something to the woman who was suffering in this time of sadness. Selfishly, I rationalized that I did not even know who had hit Kerri, only that she taught English at North, my high school.

Summer came and went, filled with flowers, grass, vacations, and twinkling laughter. But every place I turned, I saw Kerri. In people reaching out and touching each other, I saw her brand of friendship and was reminded I had not done all I could.

The first day of school that September was like all first days: filled with the cardboardy stamp of new clothes, the freshness of new textbooks and unchewed pencils, the confusion of new teachers and new faces.

Dazedly I walked into English class. Smiling questioningly, I dropped into the nearest seat, then looked up to see who my teacher was. Automatically I felt my expression turn first cold, then shocked. Mrs. Borman, the woman who had hit Kerri, was my instructor. She was young, pretty, and friendly. As my eyes met hers and I felt the helpless pain and condemnation they held, I was ashamed. I dropped my eyes, but not before Mrs. Borman had faltered momentarily and showed the hurt I had caused her.

That night when I called Sharyn and told her who my English teacher was, I heard dead silence. Finally she said softly that I had better transfer out, that I'd always blame Mrs. Borman whether I wanted to or not.

I agreed, but late that night it dawned on me that if I transferred out, my last chance to say something to Mrs. Borman would be gone. I now knew the woman, and my faith told me what should be done.

For weeks I hesitated, but I finally realized that this was a decision as important to me as to Mrs. Borman; to forgive her within myself for what was unavoidable at the time.

It was a cool, windy day in October when I walked into Mrs. B's room after school. Much like the day when they buried Kerri. But this time the bitterness was gone, and only compassion remained. In the pockets of my coat, my hands shook.

"Mrs. Borman? May I talk to you a minute?" She looked up with her sincere smile and said, "Yes, Carolyn?" I felt my facade drop as her smile melted into a look of inquiry at my expression.

I faltered. "I—I just wanted you to know that Kerri would never have blamed you, and her friend Sharyn doesn't, and I don't and nobody does and oh, please, don't feel bad."

I shut my eyes, blinking back tears and the pain I read in her face. When I met her eyes again, I couldn't take anymore. "I—I'm sorry, Mrs. B., just forget this ever happened."

Lost and terribly shaken, I began slowly walking out. Almost to the door, I heard a soft, "Carolyn."

I stopped, not turning. "Yes, Mrs. B.?" It sounded strained, hoarse.

"Carolyn—" it was a plea, for me, for others, for herself. "Carolyn, thank you."

I nodded, mutely. At the door I paused and turned. At her desk, Mrs. Borman was staring at the wall. She was a long way from North High and English, as was I. Then comprehending why healing is always painful to the Healer and those He heals, I ran.

The sky was that crazy shade of sapphire blue I'll never forget. I walked home slowly, only vaguely aware then, as before, of the cold wind blowing through my hair. Once again I remembered Kerri's bright teasing grin, those laughing, flashing walnut brown eyes; eyes that brimmed with life, love, and deep involvement everywhere she went. I felt peace, aware of the timeless understanding between hearts, needs, and souls that is friendship.

Cathy Willkie

One Dark Day

The cottage on Lake Michigan where my family and I stay for a few weeks each summer has always been a place of quiet renewal for me, where I can slow my pace and enjoy life. The lake is a keeper of life; it bathes the surrounding land in an atmosphere of aliveness you can see and feel everywhere. Each day there as I observe the harmony of wind, sand, and water, I come to believe in myself again and find my faith in God refreshed. But one day four summers ago, I learned that the lake could also bring sudden death. It was an experience which almost shattered my faith.

On that day a storm was brewing. Massive gray clouds rolled over the sun and the wind whipped the water into mountains which crashed into the shore. Swimming was too dangerous; even boats had been warned to stay off the lake. Late in the afternoon an elderly couple interested in buying the cottage stopped by to see it. We showed them around inside and then went outside to the platform at the top of the stairs, where my father pointed out the view of the lake some 50 feet below us.

Suddenly my sister Karen noticed it—an overturned cabin cruiser just offshore and two men in the water struggling to pull it to the beach. One of them, seeing us, ran to the foot of the stairs and shouted something. But we couldn't hear over the roar of the waves. Karen ran down the steps to him, and I watched, feeling a vague sense of alarm as she stiffened, turned, and bolted back up the stairs.

"There are children trapped under the boat!" she screamed. Within minutes my family, our visitors, and the minister's family next door were on the beach. The boat, belly up, was scraping on the sand, which meant we would have to lift almost its full weight to turn it over. We lined up on one side and somehow—more by willing it than by strength—we righted the huge boat.

In the jumbled mess of the forward cabin were the crumpled figures of three young boys. They were still in the orange life preservers which had kept them afloat in the air pocket under the boat, but none of them was breathing. An overpowering smell of gasoline told us the story. The boys had been able to breathe and talk to their fathers outside for a while, but then the gas fumes overcame them, and they went under, probably swallowing water and gasoline.

My father and two other men yanked the boys out by their life vests and stretched them out on the sand. People seemed to materialize out of nowhere to help as three teams started to give mouth-to-mouth resuscitation. I knelt by the head of the oldest boy, a youth of about 12 with short blond hair and delicate features. He seemed much sicker than the other two. Each time someone pushed on his stomach, he retched.

Fifteen minutes dragged by like hours. Both fathers had lapsed into shock and were unable to help. One of them crawled around on his hands and knees in the sand pleading over and over, "Please help my son, please help my son . . . ." Finally, miraculously, the two younger boys came around and started breathing on their own. The couple who had come to see the cottage were still there helping. The woman, her sleeves and pants legs rolled up, was kneeling in the sand comforting the youngest boy who was trembling and terrified.

Still the oldest boy did not respond to any of our efforts to revive him. A Coast Guard boat appeared offshore, but because of the dangerous waves and a sandbar, it couldn't come in close enough to give us the oxygen we so desperately needed. I had been praying in bits and snatches before, but now as I stood and stared helplessly at the boat, I began to pray forcefully, angrily: "God. Please, please let that boy live. Make him breathe!"

Deep inside I knew that I should really have asked God to help me accept his will, whatever it might be. But I stubbornly refused to do so. As the minutes passed and our hopes died, I could feel the bitterness start to grow in me. Finally a rescue team arrived by ambulance with oxygen, but all their efforts, like ours, failed.

I slept very little that night. Even after we went home, and the lake was not an ever-present reminder of the accident, the events of that day played over in my dreams and awakened me with the image of the dead boy's face fresh in my mind. I realize now that it was partly my own refusal to accept the tragedy that prolonged my reaction to it, but the bitterness I felt toward a God who would allow a child to die without even having had a chance to live was so strong that I could neither ignore it nor heal it myself.

One night, a week after the accident, the pattern repeated itself, and I woke up and sat up in bed suddenly. It was 2 A.M. This time I didn't fight back my fear and go back to sleep again. I just sat there feeling very empty and at the same time full to bursting with emotions I could no longer contain. I reached for my Bible lying on the night stand, flipped through it, not knowing exactly where I was going, and found myself looking down at Psalm 91.

I read it slowly, and the words reached me for the first time with the full impact of their message. "He who dwells in the shelter of the Most High will rest in the shadow of the Almighty. I will say of the Lord, 'He is my refuge and my fortress, my God, in whom I trust.' "

The tears I had held back for so long finally came; and when I finished I was no longer bitter or afraid.

To some this may not seem like a miracle, but I have never doubted that it was. The fear of death, when it grips the mind for the first time, is a power that can be shaken only by the one force which is stronger—the love of God. It was God who healed me that night. The same God who cared for three young boys and took one home with him, the same God of compassion who healed me in the moment of my greatest weakness and need so that my faith in his love would be stronger.

Sharon Johnson

The Library Incident

f I had known what was in store for me as I entered the school library that afternoon, I would have steered clear of the most embarrassing experience of my life. Just before I sat down, I noticed Jerri Hall and her friend heading for one of the smaller rooms in the library. These rooms are built in such a way that the walls do not extend all the way up to the library ceiling and people in them can often be heard talking to one another. Jerri was well aware of this and upon spotting me, she began carrying on a conversation that made my ears burn. It went like this:

"There's that Sharon Johnson. She thinks she's so neat. She's the biggest show-off there is. You should see her play basketball. She thinks she's so hot. She was showing this one girl how to do lay-ups and she couldn't even make the basket!

"Hey, Sharon Johnson," she yelled. "It's a little hard to ignore, isn't it? Are you getting angry?"

This went on and on for 10 solid minutes—the longest 10 minutes I've ever had to endure in my life. During that time I had been trying to work on an essay. But it wasn't easy to remain there in a library full of kids while I was being slandered.

I attributed Jerri's accusations to the fact that I had made the girls' basketball team and she had been cut. But that didn't make my humiliation any easier to swallow.

One other girl nearby whispered to someone, "If that were me she was talking about, I think I'd just die of embarrassment."

It appeared that I had two obvious choices to escape my embarrassing situation. The first thing I thought of was that I could walk over to Jerri and make a scene. Or I could just walk out of the library. But that would leave Jerri something more to carry on about after I'd left.

I tried to think about God's word in the Bible and how in the past it had helped me deal with difficult situations. Thanks to some of his reminders, verses I remembered from Sunday school, like, "If it is possible, as far as it depends on you, live at peace with everyone," (Rom. 12:18) and, "A gentle answer turns away wrath, but a harsh word stirs up anger," (Prov. 15:1), I gained some inner strength. It was his strength that carried me till it was time to leave and go to class.

Even so, as I left the library and escaped my persecutor, I felt miserable. Nothing is more painful than knowing that someone hates you.

I must admit Jerri's words made me see myself in a new light. Did I really show off at basketball practice? When I helped someone in basketball, was I merely taking an ego trip? My mind drifted to a sermon I'd once heard that had been about how we are often blinded to our own faults while others see them as plain as day.

Then I recalled the awful attitude I had during basketball tryouts, taking it for granted that Jerri, among others, wouldn't make the team. My expressions and behavior must have revealed my inner thoughts. I realized that God was showing me all this and I concluded that I had it coming.

Knowing that, however, wouldn't remove the bitterness that would poison our thoughts whenever Jerri and I encountered each other.

As I made my way to English, those things kept turning over in my mind. During class I felt depressed. I tried to remember the message I had read in my daily devotional booklet that morning. It had said something about God wanting me to remain confident in his infinite wisdom and allow unexplainable disturbances to draw me closer to him.

Suddenly an answer came. Why not tell Jerri how God had used her to tell me how wrong I'd been? Why not thank her for what she did and ask her to forgive me? One part of me said, "That's crazy." But the better part of me prayed, "Lord, if it's your will, give me an opportunity to do it."

I had to go to the library to finish an assignment, and the first person I saw was Jerri. I walked up to her and, trying to smile said, "Could I talk to you a minute?"

Jerri's eyes grew big and she drew back as she asked, "Why? What for?"

"Oh, I just want to talk to you about something for a minute. Please?"

I led her over to a corner room and sat down as I turned to face her.

"Look, I don't quite know how to say this, but I did a lot of thinking this afternoon. You see, I have this faith in God and I believe that he was showing me something about myself through you, something I'd never seen before. So I want to thank you for helping me to see those things. I've already asked God to forgive me but now I'd like to ask you. Apparently I've really offended you. I'm very sorry. Will you forgive me?"

Jerri, too, had a hard time finding the right words. She accepted my apology and apologized to me in return, saying that she was just kidding and didn't mean to hurt my feelings.

"Friends?" I said.

"Yeah, friends," she said with a smile.

I felt as though a crushing weight had been removed from my shoulders. It was a wonderful contented feeling.

I could now concentrate on my essay. In the process of tediously making sense out of my scrambled notes, I saw a letter addressed to me land on my table at the library. I turned to see Jerri walking out the door. The note read:

Dear Sharon,

I'd like to thank you for talking to me today in the library. You made me think and you also brought me closer to God. I want to ask you if the next time you talk to the Lord you will ask him to help me to do what's right and get along with others better.

Sincerely,

Jerri Hall.

P. S. Thank you very much!

I was so touched. And what's more, I was thrilled to see how God had worked through me in that way, to bring someone closer to him.

Brad Wilcox

Message of Love

My *lonely headlights* searched the fresh snow ahead of me. I fumbled with my top coat button against the cold. Of all nights for this to happen! Dad away in Seattle on business, and my brother Roger at college!

"Don't think about it, just drive," I told myself as the wheels slid sideways on the icy street. I tried to think of a song to fit the rhythm of the struggling windshield wipers. But there was no song in me.

No wonder it had happened. This snowstorm, the same snowfall I had thought so beautiful and pure just two hours ago, was now the white-cloaked villain who had so mercilessly forced my mother's car off the road. Now she lay unconscious in critical condition.

"Are you her son?" they had asked on the telephone.

"I'll be right there!" I had shouted.

Dad didn't know, and Rog didn't know. There was just me in my old heap of a Chevy, and this snow.

A frozen string of tears beaded my cheeks. I pulled the glove from my left hand to wipe my eyes.

Just the other day mom said these gloves were too small, I thought, as I flexed my cold fingers to circulate the blood. Are the gloves too small, or are my hands too big? These hands, which just a few hours before were squeezed so lovingly by my beautiful mother.

"That snow looks bad, mom. I wish you weren't going out tonight."

"I do, too. But some things just have to be done." She reached to squeeze my hand good-bye.

"Aw, come on, mom. I'm too old for that," I declared, withdrawing my hand. "I'm not a little boy. I don't want to play baby games any more."

"It's just my way of telling you, son. It's our secret code."

"I know, I know," I said, with exasperated resentment. "I'm tired of your silly secret code. Three squeezes, one—two—three. I love you," I mimicked in full-toned sarcasm. "Never again, mom."

The words burned in my mind as I stared blankly ahead. I could still see her hurt smile.

Three squeezes had always been our love language. Because of that simple code, countless cuts and bruises had been healed. How often had we sat in church hand-delivering our secret message, or had walked through the park saying, "I love you," in silent communication?

Mom had so many ways of showing love. "Thanks for picking me up," I would say to Mom the Chauffeur, or "You didn't have to make my bed, but thanks," to Mom the Homemaker.

"My pleasure, sir," she would respond melodramatically, squeezing my hand.

During my 16-year lifetime mom and dad must have invested a trillion hours per year just helping me. Ever since I could remember there had always been thoughtful rewards, and lately, dollar bills for feeding my gas tank or feeding my date. But always delivered with our secret code, the secret code that my hands had, only two hours ago, grown too large to return.

I clutched the steering wheel with one hand. Gripping the old glove in my teeth, I finally managed to fit it back over my chilled fingers. The snow fell lighter now. I was making better time.

I had never faced a problem entirely alone before. Rog had been the dependable big brother who always shepherded me past pitfalls, buying my lunch tickets, picking me up after practice.

I had wanted responsibility, and now I had it! *Terrified* is a pale word to describe how I felt.

What if she dies! Could anything ever be right again? Suddenly the snow looked sticky and ugly. How I wished I could bury the snow, my head, my hands, responsibility, everything!

I shifted and skidded to a stop. Several other cars slid through the snow-screened intersection. I was startled to see that the rest of the world had not stopped at the same moment my own world shattered.

The lights of the hospital guided me through the white blackness. My old car chugged, sputtered, and died. With a frustrated shove I freed the frozen door. Wind lashed at my exposed face. A slip on the ice sent me sprawling to the frozen pavement.

I stood up and shook myself. The biting wind hurried me toward the institutional glass doors.

I stammered mom's name to the receptionist. It sounded foreign. To me, she was always just "mom."

The receptionist referred to her files. She seemed ponderously slow, but finally faced me. She manipulated the switchboard, then directed me to the elevator.

"A nurse will be waiting on the third floor. I hope everything will be all right."

My rapid steps echoed dully in the endless tunnel of the hospital hallway. Elevator doors closed, trapping me inside, then drew aside again like curtains opening on a stage set. A young nurse entered stage left, taking my arm, including me in the scene.

"Please wait here," she told me. "I'll get the doctor."

I leaned my forehead against the sharp coldness of the window, peering sightlessly into the night. Snow whirled dizzily against the pane.

"Are you her son?"

I turned to find a new character in my drama. Even from my six-foot height the doctor seemed tall. Costumed in surgical green, he was well-cast in his role.

"I'm glad you came so quickly. Since your father is not here, you must be the man of the family."

I shifted uneasily in my wet shoes. Those were the exact words dad had left with me. I wanted dad here; here in the hospital where I was born, here with this tall doctor wearing this clinical face.

He led me down the hall. "This is her room. Now remember, son, you mustn't expect her to respond. She may not even recognize you. She is in a semi-conscious state and suffering considerable pain."

I pushed the door open and stepped inside. There lay a figure surrounded by machines, strapped and laced with tubes and needles. A transparent oxygen tent encompassed the upper half of the body.

As I stood looking across at that pale, pained face I realized this was not another character in my dramatic scene. This was my mother!

Mom's eyes opened in an unnatural stare. I stepped across the silence of that small hospital room lit only by street lamps outside the window. I reached out and laid my trembling hand on hers. I knew what I had to do. My message had to be clear. I squeezed—one-two-three. Only God knew how important it was that she understand.

Her eyes flickered. She knew me! A tear ran down my face and dropped upon my hand—the hand that had been too grownup for this baby game.

My hand enfolded hers and passed our secret code again and again until she fell asleep. Through the window I could see the snow falling gently now.

"Thank you," I prayed in marvelous relief. "Thank you for life, and hands, and secret codes."

G. Alan Von Stein

Hard Decision

When *God* closes one door, he opens another." I'd heard that expression many times, but I'd never thought about its meaning until a door in my life slammed abruptly shut.

Late in September one year, our Wynford Royal football team took the field against our league rival River Valley Vikings. I was a junior returning letterman, and I was psyched for the game. I played both ways at the fullback and linebacker slots, and my whole life revolved around football. I practiced, slept, and dreamed football, and I was thoroughly convinced I could get a full ride to some small college on a football scholarship.

The game started promptly at 8:00 P.M. Team members on both sides played with great intensity, and I was no exception. The first quarter I had eight tackles, four of which were solos. I really thought I was invincible.

Early in the second quarter, we were on defense, and my good fortune continued until a third-down play that turned out to be the most important play of my career. River Valley snapped the ball. The quarterback pitched the ball

to the tailback, and I started in hot pursuit. I was about 10 yards from the ball carrier when I felt a tremendous hit on my left leg. Everything in my left knee seemed to snap, and I went down instantly. I felt little pain, but I knew I shouldn't get up. The referee came over and said, "Are you hurt, son?" I calmly answered, "Yes." He then motioned to the sidelines for help, and my coaches and the team doctor were soon working on my leg. When the doctor moved my knee from side to side, it felt like it wasn't attached to the rest of my body. He moved it as if it were rubber.

I was helped from the field so the doctor could examine me more closely. I wasn't acquainted with the team doctor, but I somehow felt comfortable with him, I asked him how badly I was hurt, and he told me that I was out for the season. The tears came. I realized not playing a full year as a junior would mean no conference honors and probably no scholarship.

The doctor said I had to go to the hospital but I shouldn't have to stay any longer than overnight. As I was taken away in the ambulance my teammates promised me they would win the game for me. This really brought the tears.

When I arrived at the hospital, my parents were there. They warned me not to count on getting released the next day. Apparently they knew something I didn't.

The next day my doctor took me to have X-rays. After the X-rays were read, he asked me what I would say if he suggested I have surgery. I said, "If that is what it takes to get well and play football again, I'll have the surgery."

I wasn't afraid of the operation. I don't know why. Maybe it was because my pastor came and prayed with me before surgery, or maybe it was because I didn't realize how badly I was hurt.

I went into surgery on Monday, October 1, at 1:00 P.M. and I was in surgery until 5:00 P.M. After the operation, my surgeon came out and told my parents the extent of the injury. He said I had torn most of my ligaments, muscles, nerves, and the hamstring in my left knee. He also said that the surgery went well, but he couldn't promise that I wouldn't be crippled for the rest of my life.

The doctor kept me and my newly acquired leg-length cast in the hospital for 10 days. Those 10 days were very long, although I did have many visitors to keep me company. However, when I went home, the number of visitors slowly decreased, and I began to think about my operation.

I became very depressed and irritable. I prayed many times, asking God, "Why did this have to happen to me? I've been good."

I became even more frustrated when I returned to school and had to cope with carrying my books, climbing stairs, and watching other kids participate in sports. I grew very bitter and I spent much time praying, trying to find out, "Why me?" However, through all this time of pain and frustration, the one thing I never resented was football. Instead I thought only of playing next year.

At the end of eight weeks, my cast was removed, and I was fitted with a $300 Joe Namath brace, which I was to wear for 18 months, 24 hours a day.

Now the work really began. I spent many hours lifting weights, running, and jumping rope. The exercises were painful, but I knew if I wanted to play football next year, I would have to discipline and dedicate myself to the task of rebuilding my leg. And I did want to play!

After seven months of rehabilitation, my knee was tested for strength and was found to be 102 percent as strong as my good leg. Unfortunately, it was not as stable. I then went to my surgeon, and he told me that if I played, I risked injury that would probably leave me crippled. But the final decision about returning to football was mine.

I spent many hours weighing the pros of playing and spent many hours praying for guidance. More than any other time in my life, I examined my priorities. More than any other time, I prayed to God to show me his will. With his help, I made my decision not to play football my senior year.

It was very hard to watch my teammates play this past season. I missed the excitement and the glory. I missed being part of a winning team. But the players all understood and praised my decision not to take the chance of being crippled for life.

Not everything has turned out badly for me; in fact, I think God opened many new doors for me. I feel I have developed new interests and have become more understanding of others' pain. In fact, I was so impressed with my surgeon that I have now decided to major in premedicine and hope to help injured athletes as my surgeon has helped me. It was painful to have the door to my high school football career close, but I now understand that when one door in life closes, another opens. I hope I have learned to recognize those open doors—to use the opportunities in life rather than to be bitter about lost chances. Maybe this is the answer to my question, "Why me?"

Jonathan Alexander

The Big Wave

One day in the not too long ago past I experienced something so powerful, so moving, so unexplainable that it could only be termed religious. It has changed my life and me, not outwardly perhaps, but inwardly—emotionally.

It was a summer day, and I was at Leo Carrillo Beach with a few of my friends. I live in southern California, so during the summer we often spend a great deal of our time on the sand or body surfing in the waves.

There's really nothing quite like getting out in the ocean—way out, where one good swell, one big wave, can pick you off the ocean floor and let you tread water for four, maybe five minutes. Then, when the right wave comes along, not too big, but not too small, you turn toward the shore and swim just as fast as you can. If you catch the wave right, if you're on the wave's face just as it starts to break, that's where the real fun begins. The wave, only a tiny stroke of the giant ocean, thrusts you toward the shore, forcefully yet carefully, and leaves you lying contentedly on the wet beach sand.

Body surfing, however, is not always so simple. There are times when, while you are trying to swim out through the cold water, the waves break directly on top of you. Or sometimes you don't judge the water wall just right, and instead of riding the top of the wave you end up being churned and tumbled inside of it. This is not a pleasant experience, but it's all part of the sport, and surviving a tough wipeout is just as gratifying, and probably worth more stories, than getting a good ride.

The waves this bright summer day were unusually big, probably due to some offshore storm. When I went into the water for the fifth time, the sun had dropped low in the sky, moving closer to the water-filled horizon. I swam out easily past where the waves were breaking 30 yards or more off the shoreline.

I wasn't bobbing long when I spotted a nice, big wave building up about 20 yards farther out. I yelled to my friend John, who was in the water about 15 feet to my left. He nodded and yelled back that the wave looked "real good." We turned toward the shore and started swimming simultaneously, just like two little water ballerinas or something. I swam as hard as I could, as fast as I could, furiously trying to get in position for the oncoming wave.

I felt the wave swell under me. I felt it lift me up and begin to push me forward. I glanced across at John, and I saw that he too had caught it. But just as I looked over at him, he yelled, "No way!" and he turned back over the top of the wave—just as it began to break.

I looked down, for now I had glided up to the top of the wave, and all that I could see was wet sand below, way below. There was a slight riptide that day, a tide that pulled the water back out to sea much quicker than usual. The water from the previous waves had receded into the foot of my wave, leaving it twice as tall as the others. I wanted to back up, but it was too late. The wave had already started to break, and I couldn't possibly turn back without getting torn apart by the hard, blue wall.

Now, I have been hit by many a wave in my day, but nothing I have ever felt compared to the way this wave smashed me. It pounded me into the hard, wet sand, and then it spun me and churned me, as if trying to tear my limbs from my body. On other tough waves, I'd known what to do: Stay close to the bottom, wait for the wave to pass, then push to the surface.

So I waited for what seemed like a decade but was actually only about 15 seconds. Finally, when the turbulence ceased, I regained my balance and pushed for the surface. But this time, for the first time in my life, the push failed to get me to the top. I was submerged about three feet below the surface of the water and three feet off the bottom. I had no energy left, and I was out of breath. I began to flap about, but I soon realized that effort was to no avail.

I looked up, toward the surface, resigned suddenly that I was about to die. There, on the outer layer of the water, I saw the sunlight sparkling like little golden stars. Those little stars came to me as some sort of sign. Whether this sign came from without or within, I cannot say, but I recognized it as a sign of God, a sign of love, a sign of truth. And immediately, despite being on the verge of drowning, on the verge of death, I was at peace, and I was at ease with the thought of dying. That was what my religious experience was, and still is, all about. At what I believed was my moment of death, a sign was given to me, a sign that told me that death was not evil, but good; and that I should not fear, for I would be protected. It was a feeling of pleasure, not pain; of gain, not loss.

How I escaped my death, I really don't know, I can't even remember surfacing, or that first gasp of air. All I recall is that somehow I staggered onto the beach, and that John helped pull me up and walk me to the car. To this day I do not know how, or why, I lived through that ordeal, for at the time I thought that only a small miracle could keep me alive.

Yet now I approach life from a different standpoint. I have seen death, and it is not bad at all. I am no longer afraid to die, and thus I am no longer afraid to live. Those two go hand-in-hand. And, in that God has confirmed the goodness of death to me, so has he confirmed the goodness of life.

Krista Rogers

Nobody Whispered in My Ear

I think it's time for those tonsils to come out." I could still hear Dr. Baker's words as I threw my pajamas into the suitcase. *Why me? I hate hospitals.*

I looked at my list. Toothbrush. I ran into the bathroom to get it. I banged the cabinet shut and turned around so fast I nearly knocked over my little sister, who was standing in the doorway.

"Hi, Pumpkin," I said. "How was kindergarten today?" I brushed her aside, not waiting for her answer.

"How did you say school was?" I asked, seeing that Mary had followed me. She answered so quietly I could hardly hear her. "What did you say?" I whispered with a smile, imitating her voice.

"I said we didn't do anything fun." She spoke louder, annoyed that she had to repeat herself.

"Didn't you get to color?" I asked, stuffing my slippers into the suitcase.

"Yes," she said, pushing a wisp of hair out of her eyes, "but they wouldn't let me go in the playhouse." Her bright eyes seemed unusually sad.

"What's wrong, Mary?" I asked.

"Nobody whispered in my ear today and said they want to be my friend."

"Nobody what?" I asked, suddenly realizing how serious she was.

"Nobody whispered in my ear today and said they want to be my friend," she repeated sadly. Her eyes glistened.

"Don't worry, Mary," I said, feeling a sudden flash of indignation. "Those mean kids just don't know what a sweet girl you are." I tweaked her nose, gave her a smile, and returned to my packing. Wiping her eyes with her little fists, she left the room.

At 7:00 P.M. I followed dad into the hospital, so scared that my stomach was in knots. The place was enormous, ghostly white, and smelled of alcohol. Fluorescent lights hummed, and I shivered.

After the extended routine of papers, temperatures, and blood tests, I was ready for my room. Shrouded in apprehension and with butterflies still in my stomach, I gave dad a hug and entered the room alone. It seemed colder than the hall. I glanced curiously around the room, the pale walls, the sink, the window, but stopped suddenly upon seeing the patient in the next bed. I looked quickly away. I was already nervous, but seeing her made me more so.

Her name was Jennifer Redd. I knew her, or at least her reputation. I moved cautiously across the shiny floor. I had no intention of recognizing her. She had been expelled from school. I wasn't sure why, but one of my friends said she was heavily into drugs. Purposely sitting with my back to her, I put away my belongings. At school I had often passed her in D-wing. She'd hang out there with a bunch of rough, troublemaking kids. We called them "the parking lot gang."

I glanced at her. She was looking squarely at me, almost glaring. I looked away. She smoked a lot; I knew that wasn't rumor. There was hardly a time I had seen her without a cigarette, the smoke drifting up to nest in her peroxided hair—and that blue eye shadow.

I wondered if she recognized me. We were in the same health class once, but I'd never gotten to know her; I'd never really had a desire to. People like her frightened me. I somehow felt that if I was her friend, I would become like her.

I turned on the TV, which I kept on all evening, trying to avoid another eye encounter. I was relieved when a nurse told us it was time for sleep. I slipped into the bathroom and into my pajamas, then returned to snuggle under my blankets like a cocoon.

I woke up, straining to remember where I was. Dim yellow light from the hall made shadowed shapes around me. The surroundings were eerie, unfamiliar, and I wanted to be home in my own bed. I fumbled for my watch on the night stand, wondering how long I had slept.

"It's two A.M." I jerked around, startled by Jennifer's voice. She laughed, knowing that she had frightened me.

"You can't sleep either?" she asked. I shook my head, and she continued almost eagerly.

"I hate bein' cooped up here for a weekend. Friday night is party night for the gang." Her voice trailed on. I don't think she cared if I was there or not.

"They tried to catch me with some drugs once," she laughed. "But I fooled 'em." Her life-style disgusted me. How could she enjoy such stupid things? Then she sat up, tossed her head, and arched her eyebrows.

"Got a cigarette?"

"No," I answered, "I don't smoke."

"Oh, you don't smoke." She mimicked the way I said it, making me sound like a goody two-shoes.

"Doesn't matter," she said, "I'll find a way to get some." She continued talking, almost bragging about all the things she'd done. I wanted to get out of bed, go over, shake her and say, "Look what you're doing to yourself." I felt like a mother.

"You should have seen what we did to a kid's new car," she laughed. I couldn't stand it any longer.

"Why do you do these things, Jennifer?" I burst out, interrupting her. I sat up. "Why do you live like this?"

She sat cross-legged, staring at me, her bare knees sticking out from under her blue nightgown. She looked almost like a little girl . . . like Mary, I thought. Then her expression changed and she lashed out at me.

"You want to know why I'm like this? You really want to know?" Her eyes were blazing and her whole body trembled. I was suddenly afraid to know.

"I'll tell you why, Miss High and Mighty," she said. "It's because you wouldn't accept me." Her words were like a slap in my face. I sat there stunned . . . and I kept seeing Mary's sad face. I looked at Jennifer and almost waited for her to say, "Nobody whispered in my ear today. . . ." But she just turned her back to me.

I watched the shadows shift dark and light. It was all so clear now. I was one of those mean kids in her class.

Agonizing minutes passed before I stepped over, reached out, and touched her shoulder

"Jennifer," I whispered, "I'm sorry."

"It's all right, kid," she said, not looking up. "Don't worry about me."

But, back in my bed, I knew I would worry. I cried hot tears into my pillow. "Please, God, forgive me," I sobbed. "I'll never be cruel again."

Hours passed; I don't know how many. I turned my damp pillow over and sat up. Light was coming in the window now, and suddenly I realized the ache was gone, and in it's place, a calmness. Now I thanked God for giving me a second chance, and I thought of all the kids at school who could start counting on me.

Kandi Isaacs

The Fun of Being Me

hen our pastor asked me if I would sing a "special" in church sometime, I grinned to myself. It was amusing to think that only one year before I would have cringed at getting up in front of people. I accepted his offer and we set a date.

Soon I decided I needed a new dress for the occasion. So the next Saturday I collected enough courage to fight the crowds and drove to a nearby department store.

Much to my surprise I quickly found four dresses I really liked. Little did I know that these four dresses would be used to show me something very important about myself. In the fitting room, my mind began to review the changes in me in the past year. It was hard to believe and impossible to conceive how in seven short months I could have lost 60 pounds.

How unbelievable this miracle was. Even more unbelievable was that God would care enough about me to send his strength and love to help make it possible.

I picked up the red dress and took it off the hanger. As I began to put it on, the red color glared at me in the mirror, and my mind seemed to revert back to my childhood. . . .

I was always a heavy child, and it seemed that the jeers of "Fatty, fatty, two by four" were always around to upset me. One day, in junior high, I returned from lunch early, and as I turned a corner, I heard two boys' voices coming from a room.

"She's so fat! I didn't know they made ugliness in her size," chuckled one boy.

"Well, they do!"

I couldn't believe how cruel they were being. I really felt sorry for whoever the girl was they were talking about, and I was going to tell them so! Just before I jerked the door open, I heard more. Too much more.

"No wonder they call her Kandi—she eats too much of it, I guess!"

Laughter filled the room, but just behind the door, I stood in shock. My stomach felt as if it had been stabbed and the pain shot through my body. As my pulse raced and I grew whiter and whiter, the other students returned from lunch. Pretending nothing was wrong, I entered the classroom and took my seat. I felt a pain so deep that, although no one saw it, its cutting edge carved feelings of inferiority in me that would last for years.

I began to withdraw more and more. I didn't go to the games at school or the skating rink as other kids my age did. I was so afraid of what people thought of me, and I couldn't bear to be hurt again. If I could just get away from people, my problem would be solved, I thought. But how could I escape from myself? I still cried every time I passed a full-length mirror or outgrew another size. . . .

Now, in the dressing room of the department store, I found myself staring at the red dress I'd put on. It made me remember a bright red skirt I had broken a zipper on once. I quickly took the dress off and swallowed hard to keep from crying. I felt that horrid pain again. As soon as the dress was off, the memories stopped. It was almost as if the dress was *causing* the memories.

I replaced it on the hanger and reached for another dress, a blue one. I slipped it over my head, and as the soft blue passed my eyes, I realized that the shade was the exact color of our church interior. My mind began to take another journey, this time to a Christmas night at our church. . . .

As I sat quietly, I saw several people walk forward to the altar and kneel to pray. All of a sudden I felt a pulling toward the altar. It was as if a rope had come from the altar and wrapped itself around my heart, and if I didn't go forward, my heart would be jerked from my body. I slowly stood and walked to the front of the church. As I knelt there, a strange feeling came over me. A ball of fire seemed to burn in my heart. The more I cried, the more it burned.

"Lord," I prayed, "please help me. I feel so lonely and rejected. You're the only one I can turn to, and I know you can change things. Please help me." Suddenly, the ball of fire in my heart stopped burning and turned to a warm liquid. The ball exploded and the liquid seemed to flow all over me. I had reached that famous "peace that passeth understanding."

When I returned to my pew, I was totally filled with Christ's love and I knew he cared for me. I truly knew now that when he suffered and died on that cross, it was for me. I also knew deep inside that I had found the answer to my weight problem. I knew I had the strength to do it and God would help me.

It's hard to believe such a decision could be made in such short time, but isn't that how God works? All he's waiting on is for us to come to the end of ourselves and call on him. . . .

"Assistance in cosmetics, please!"

The voice over the loudspeaker brought me back to the department store dressing room. I slipped out of the blue dress, and the scene of the church disappeared from my mind. Next, I reached for the green dress. The tiny yellow flowers sprinkled over it reminded me of fresh springtime. By now I had become accustomed to the trips down memory lane that my mind was taking each time I put on a different dress. So I sat down on the bench and waited for the next adventure. . . .

It was spring. Seven months is a long time to stay on a diet, and it had taken willpower and much prayer. I was still losing, but for the first time in my life, I felt at ease and comfortable about my weight.

Before too long, I began coming out of my shell. I began to be active in the youth group at church and have fun with other kids socially. At the end of that school year, I was voted "most talented" and more surprising, I was nominated for "best dressed."

God had become very real to me during this time, and I knew him truly as my Heavenly Father who withholds no good thing from his children. Realizing who I am in Christ had given me the courage to be the unique person he had made me. I was now free to live and enjoy life. I had new courage. In high school, I ran for class treasurer and student council president, both of which I won. My impossible dream had come true; not to be loved by my peers, but to love myself enough to reach out to others. . . .

Shaking myself, I once again returned to the dressing room, and began to put on the last dress. Where would my mind travel this time? The dress was solid white, but there was something mysterious about it. After glancing in the mirror, I sat down on the bench and waited. Nothing happened. I continued to wait. Still nothing happened.

"God," I whispered, "I know you had a reason for walking me through those three periods of my life, but what is the dress for? Is there more?" Then his answer came clearly.

"This dress can be whatever you choose," he said. "This white dress represents the future with its unblemished potential for success and happiness. You have the option of choosing that bright but uncertain future or living by your past failure. The choice is yours."

With a knowing smile, I slipped my own clothes back on and, with the white dress in my hand, approached the check-out counter.

"Yes, Lord," I prayed, "I choose the future with all its mystery and uncertainty because I know that whatever lies waiting over the next hill isn't too big for you and me to handle together."

Teresa Schantz

Lori and Me

My mind was still caught up in vacation excitement as I walked off the plane into the Kansas City airport, exchanged hugs with my parents, and tried to answer all the questions they threw out at me. I'd been away visiting my cousins for a few weeks.

"Gosh, it's going to be great to see Lori," I interjected, referring to my best friend. Two loners, Lori Dailey and I met in the seventh grade. We fast discovered that together we could attack life and its problems and win. A rare friendship developed in which neither of us was the "leader" but instead we shared decisions and talents. I think our love for each other was an echo of a verse from 1 Samuel 18:1: "Jonathan became one in spirit with David, and he loved him as himself."

Mom spoke softly. "I think Lori really misses you, too. You see, she's had kind of a shock. There was a fire. Lori's home is partly destroyed."

Now I was scared for Lori. For indeed, the fire had all but ruined the Daileys' home. Its first flickers had rapidly enveloped the kitchen. Later, as I walked through the ruins,

I found nothing of the colorful, woodsy room so familiar to me. The kitchen now resembled a tomb with its black, charred walls; only ashes remained where appliances and furniture had stood. The phone on the wall had melted, and the plastic had oozed down, desperately clinging to the wall. Lori's room had the air of having been caught by surprise. Clothes still lay where she had tossed them on the bed; it was spooky.

It was many months before the Daileys found a new home and slowly replaced the necessities. Their church and friends helped with many prayers and various donations.

Although it had been a terrible experience, to my surprise it wasn't Lori who was hurt by the tragedy—but me! A gnawing feeling took over the pit of my stomach. Though I had been a lifelong Christian, Lori had only become a Christian during our freshman year in high school. Now, because of the fire, Lori had a new-found strength that I felt lacking in myself. People's incessant interest in Lori and her needs began to irritate me. I found myself standing, puzzled, before a wall of jealousy. Could I actually be jealous of Lori's fire?

Talking to Lori one afternoon, I found that the fire had actually increased her peace of mind and rearranged her priorities.

"When something like a fire happens," she said, "you find out that things really don't matter that much to you."

Looking around my own spacious room bursting with things—records, music, a desk my father had made me, pictures, sentimental mementos and awards—I felt like a bumbling hippo wallowing in selfishness. To have these objects destroyed would really hurt me, I knew. They seemed like an important part of me.

I think it was on that day that I realized what was wrong with me. Lori's young faith had been tested, and she had come through the winner. The faith I'd felt secure in had never really been tested. Now, I found myself almost wishing that something terrible would happen so that I could experience what Lori had.

My life seemed so ordinary. My father and both grandfathers being Christians, my faith had come naturally to me. Our family had experienced no gruesome deaths or horrifying accidents. My life had been woven with the various experiences of a preacher's home—both good and bad—and they had made me strong. Or, at least, I had thought so. But my life had lacked the dramatic incident that would set me apart from the crowds of average Christians.

Everything about my life had been too simple, too perfect—frighteningly so. Luke 12:48 now became almost a threat: "From everyone who has been given much, much will be demanded." Was the Lord going to be terribly severe with me because he had given me so much and had allowed me to be so protected from tragedy?

Then one day my dad made a statement in a sermon that helped me. He said, "The great people are those who believe that nothing is ordinary. Every person, every job, every time, and every place is very special. And because they really believe this, life for them, in fact, becomes extraordinary."

It made me ask myself, "What's wrong with being ordinary?" Must I do great evil in order to come back and find God? Was my faith puny because I was reared in a Christian home with few of the labor pains of growing up in a sinful world? Was I inferior spiritually because I had no dramatic story of faith to tell? Should I be ashamed of good health and a happy home?

So, strangely, Lori's fire brought spiritual victory not just to her, but to me. For the first time I really appreciated being just an ordinary person with no exciting experience to tell. Being an average person is a great blessing. For the ordinary person can, by God's power, be the most powerful force of all—a simple life used faithfully for his glory.

Mike Verde

A Better Discovery than Oil

Until last summer I thought being successful meant having a prestigious job, hordes of money, and great fame. During a 10-day period my grandpa taught me a new definition, the one God has in mind for us. Strangely enough, grandpa did so without ever saying a word.

"Now, son," grandpa said (he always begins a serious talk that way), "this country ain't gonna collapse if something should go wrong with this oil field. It don't produce no thousand barrels a week, but, son, they hired me to be darn sure that it produces all the oil it can. As long as the good Lord sustains my health, that's exactly what I'm gonna do. I expect you to do the same."

"Grandpa, would you quit worrying," I said. "You've gone over everything I'll need to do a 100 times."

For five days Grandpa drilled me on every detail of what I was supposed to do around the oil field, while he was gone on his first vacation in 10 years. He took great pride in maintaining that oil field, which was really no more than three weathered tanks and seven miniature pumps. I thought his duties were rather simple, but I never told him that.

Once, near the end of my five-day learning session, I tried to teach Grandpa a new way to figure the oil charts that he maintained, by using algebraic principles. He was very impressed, but the concept totally confused him.

"Son," he said, "your grandpa ain't no Alfred Einstein when it comes to math. You must be pretty smart though, boy, to know how to mix them letters and numbers to get the right answer. They teach you that in school?"

"Yes, sir," I answered. "But it's Albert Einstein, grandpa, not Alfred."

"Well, I ain't him neither." We both laughed.

While grandpa followed the ruts his little Datsun truck had made over the years around the oil field, constantly reminding me which valves to turn on and which to turn off, I wondered what he had been like when he was a boy. Apparently Charlie Leonard—that is his other name—was not anything like me. I wanted to make something of my life, to be somebody special, and to do something worthwhile. Grandpa seemed so content just spending his days working in the oil field. I could not understand. I finally decided that he had never been as ambitious as I was.

I was glad when the day finally came for grandpa to leave. For the next 10 days I would have his house and the oil field all to myself. I figured it would be easy to fill grandpa's shoes; I was wrong.

The first morning I was making the routine rounds checking the pumps when I spotted a truck parked by one of the tanks. Not recognizing the vehicle, I drove over to investigate.

"Good morning, sir, can I help you?"

"You must be Charlie's grandson," the man said.

"Yes, sir, I am. Who are you?"

He got out of his truck and walked over to me and extended his hand. "The name's Claude Waldrop; I'm Charlie's foreman."

"You mean my grandpa works for you?" I asked.

"Well, officially he does, but ol' Charlie knows 10 times more about this oil field than I do."

How could my grandpa work for a younger man? I thought. It was obvious that I was embarrassed.

"You've got a lot to be proud of in your grandfather," the man said. "He's one of the finest Christian men I know. I think Charlie would help the devil himself. That's just the way he is, always helping others."

I figured Mr. Waldrop was just trying to be nice. My grandpa was just an oil-field worker; certainly Mr. Waldrop knew finer men by the world's standards.

"Thank you," I said halfheartedly.

After I gauged the amount of oil in the tanks, I drove home to call in the information. Promptly at 8 A.M., as instructed, I made my morning call to the main office.

A lady answered the phone.

"Good morning," I said. "I'm calling in Charlie Leonard's daily oil reports."

"Oh," the female voice shot back excitedly, "you must be Mike."

"Yes, ma'am," I said. "How did you know?"

"Your grandfather always talks about you, Mike. He really loves you. To tell you the truth, I don't know anyone your grandfather doesn't love. Whenever I'm feeling down, he'll say, 'Now, Bea, God's Word says, "All things work together for the good of them that love the Lord."' He always encourages me to place my faith in God. I don't know what I'd do without him."

Grandpa never told me about that part of his job. Slowly I was beginning to understand what he really did for a living.

That same evening, while watching television, I heard a feeble knock on the door. Opening the door, I saw a gray-haired, withered old woman.

"Who are you?" the lady's voice cracked.

"I'm Charlie Leonard's grandson," I said. "I'm tending to his job while he's away."

"Well," she mumbled, "I sure hope the doctors can find out what's wrong."

I was confused. I knew for certain that grandpa was not seeing any doctors; he was on a vacation.

The old lady's eyes appeared dazed; they moved aimlessly back and forth. Suddenly, I knew that it was she who was confused, for this was the neighbor grandpa had told me about before he left. He said she was pleasantly senile, had been ever since her husband died. He asked me to speak to her every day. He said a kind word was the best medicine for loneliness.

"I'm sure he'll be fine," I said.

Her eyes started to water. "I hope so," she said, "he's about all I got left."

I realized then that my grandpa did not just spend his days fiddling around some forgotten oil patch. He invested his time in a more precious product—people. I had already met three who had been blessed by his investment, and as the days passed I met others.

There was the grocer whose son would not have been able to attend an out-of-state church retreat if grandpa hadn't paid his way. There was the young man grandpa worked with each day for four years teaching him how to kick a football. The boy later attended college on a football scholarship. Every day I met someone whose life had been blessed by Charlie Leonard, and I was proud.

The day grandpa returned, I rushed to meet him. I hugged him before he could get out of the car. "Grandpa," I exclaimed, "you're the greatest man I know!"

"Thank you, son," he said, "but I just produce oil."

"No, grandpa," I answered, "you produce love, a thousand barrels a week."

As I carried in his luggage, I dreamed of being as successful as my grandpa someday.

Success to me now is having a job helping others, hordes of friends, and a great faith in God.

John C. Gregg

Before I Forget . . .

Grandma sat absorbed, arranging and rearranging the silverware on her flowered placemat. Suddenly she looked up, smiled brightly and said, "She is heavy work . . . will let us know." Realizing that what she had meant to say had not come out right, she dropped her head in embarrassment and confusion, only to raise it again to say, "I want to lie down. Coming, grandpa?" Before we could recover and encourage her to finish her meal with us, she had risen and wandered off, her destination already forgotten.

At 72 my grandma, Vlasta Ott, is a victim of Alzheimer's disease. Her brain has already lost its capacity to locate the bathroom in our house. Thoughts get trapped in the tangling nerve branches—lost—unable to be verbalized. Once brilliant and fluent in five languages, she sees her skills and memory slipping away—slowly enough for her to comprehend what is happening to her. This must be the worst part, knowing with icy certainty what terrible thing is going to befall you and not being able to do anything about it.

I feel afraid for her, but I can only imagine what it must be like. Contact with the world I have known would begin to fade—seeing what is around me but being unable to make sense of what was once familiar.

One evening I was helping to set the table. My grandmother hovered like a pale, frail moth at my elbow. She gravitated toward my activity as a moth moves toward light, seeking brightness and warmth, ignorant of the danger. "All we need are two more, grandma," I said, gesturing toward the bowls in the cabinet. Her hand started for the bowls, but suddenly headed for the glasses, ordered by some unseen force—unable to make the right choice. Her look of pleading confusion, almost causing me to cry, instantly disappeared as a new thought entered her short-circuiting brain. Purposeful activity was lost, and she attempted to organize several napkins, her hands shaking with uncertainty.

Those hands had once chosen books for me, volumes we would sit and read together. Those bright blue eyes had lovingly acknowledged my interest. Those ears had listened to my expressions of joy, my howling anger. She had chosen to love me.

Grandma made other choices for love in her life. She raised three girls, helping each to discover unique talents. She chose to teach: those who wanted to learn a language, those who were forced to stay in the hospital, those who were handicapped. She chose to share her enthusiasm, her electric sense of humor, and her versatile teaching style with those whom she nurtured. She saw their potential, nourished their particular strengths, and set them free to make choices of their own. She had given love, hope, and life. How could a loving God, who gives us choices, suddenly pass my grandmother by?

We sat around the breakfast table—my mother, grandmother, and I. Grandma looked tired, but for a moment she was lucid. My mother commented, "It's hard when you understand what we're saying but can't tell us what you think."

"Yes," grandma replied. "Sometimes I try to say things fast. I want to get them out before I forget, but it doesn't work." She sighed and looked into my mother's eyes. "I would not have chosen this end for myself, but it's what I've been given."

My mother began to weep. Grandma reached out to her, gathering her daughter in her arms to comfort her once again.

My grandmother's time to choose is coming to an end. Her last choice is to accept the suffering that has been given her and make the best of it, as she always has. God never promised that we would not suffer, only that he would always be with us if we trusted him. God's Son accepted suffering and death in order to give us new life. Though grandma's life is ending in darkness, she will live on in the love and goodness she so freely gave to me and to others. She made good use of her choices.

One birthday long ago my grandmother gave me a present that would eventually be used for my college education. I was overwhelmed by her generous gift and felt unworthy. "How can I ever repay you, grandma?" I mumbled while looking at my shoelaces.

She lifted my chin so that our eyes met and said, "Your job is not to pay me back, John. Pass it on."

I will, grandma. Thank you.

Carole Lynn Douglas

To Love the Imperfect

It wasn't a minister, youth leader, a close friend, or even a parent who strengthened my faith in God. It was my brain-injured sister.

Mary was a year old when she became ill with sleeping sickness. It took her a long time to recover, but she finally made it one year later when I was born. As far back as I can remember there seemed to be no love or understanding between Mary and me. At the age of seven I had a dislike for everyone; I was jealous because I thought Mary received more attention, and resentful since I felt that God had no right to burden me with a retarded sister. She couldn't read or write, nor could she talk about anything more than the simple wants of life.

During my elementary years I confess that I was an unhappy, mean, and jealous "brat." This was probably because during those first years I was left alone a lot while mother took care of Mary's demands. Mary would run to meet me when I came home from school and I would try to get away from her. I was ashamed to be seen with her uptown. I almost wished that she would die.

I was told in Sunday school to "love my neighbor" and to have compassion for little children and to believe in God, but to my child's mind those were just good ideas to talk about, not to live by. Faith did not come easily to me. I never would have made it without Mary.

The change probably began the first night I heard Mary's prayers as she sat on the stairway before she went to bed. They went like this: "Bless mama and daddy and my sister Carole. Make her love me. I love her. Bless my dinner and my bed and thank you for Blondie and my kittens, Radar and Snagglepuss. Help me be a good girl and, God, I want to come up in heaven with you."

Mary's faith remained simple and small like a grain of mustard seed. Gradually, however, her trust became more firmly embedded and the prayers on the staircase became longer. Some of the prayers had a real spark of beauty.

One summer on her birthday, Mary cried for a Bible. I already had had one for three years, but no one had ever bought Mary one as she couldn't read. So I went to the store and found a little white Bible full of pictures. Mary took it to church every Sunday. At home she looked at the pictures and wanted mother and me to tell her stories to go with the pictures.

I noticed that mother made the stories simple and that she always stressed faith in a Christ who lives today. About the picture of Jesus on the cross she explained, "No, Jesus isn't on the cross any more. That was a long time ago. Now he's alive and taking care of us."

Then she would show Mary the picture of the ascension. As Mary's simple faith grew, so did mine. Today there is no question in Mary's mind but that God is up in heaven taking care of everyone and everything she loves, including her pets and toys and furniture.

One day when I was in seventh grade, someone taunted me with, "You've got a sister in the dummy class. Ha! Ha!" I felt like wilting but I whispered a prayer instead. Then before I knew it, I was saying, "God loves everyone, black or white, dumb or smart. He even loves you, but you don't act as if you knew it."

Faith has helped me and no one has ever again made fun of me for my sister's imperfections.

Recently I visited an aunt and as I was looking through her new picture window across the beautiful corn shucks in the field and beyond to the yellow and saffron and scarlet covered hills, my aunt said that she wished the old tumble-down barn in the middle of the picture didn't spoil the view. An idea enveloped me—perhaps God sent it. I remarked, "That's what makes the view complete. Life isn't all glorious, all beautiful. I really like the imperfect things. The shabbiness and imperfections of the broken-down barn make the rest of the scene more beautiful by contrast."

So it is with my imperfect sister. She cannot read; yet her faith is strong. She helps complete our family picture. God has used Mary to make my faith in him much larger than a mustard seed. Now when Mary prays on the stairway I can feel God's warmth and presence.

Yes, the meaning of life has been revealed to me through a retarded sister. I know now that I really do love imperfect and problem children and adults as well. They are real children of God and he is using them to generate faith in those of us with little faith.

Kathleen Roy

What Really Matters?

I was already late for the bus. The hill I had to go down was so steep that I had to move extra slowly. My books were heavy and my muscles cramped as I carried the load. At last, the hill behind me, I could see the bus stop where the ground leveled, and I knew that this morning I would reach my destination without falling.

"Hi, Kath," said my friend.

"Hi. Sure is cold this morning."

As we began to talk, I automatically concentrated on our conversation instead of my balance. A book fell from my arms as I lurched a little.

"Here, Silly," my pal said affectionately as he handed it back to me. We crowded into the bus and I almost lost my balance as I walked down the aisle. But in my seat at last, I was safely on my way to school.

When the bus stopped I went to my locker and finally dropped my heavy load. "Good morning, Mr. Dell." He was my English teacher—and one of my favorites.

"Well, Kathy, how's my friend today?" he asked.

"Okay," I answered. I went on to my homeroom.

As I walked down the hall, I felt my legs turn in as they always do when I try to move faster. My spastic movements were noticed by my schoolmates but they, as I, have grown used to them. The brain damage I suffered at birth has left me with cerebral palsy, which has affected my speech and motor control, and maneuvering the crowded school halls is difficult for me. But what's a handicap anyway when God is at your side!

As I entered my homeroom, I laughed at a joke a classmate told me. "You're a nut," I said to him.

"That's true, but I'm not half as nutty as you," he said.

"Well, you're runnin' a close second," I remarked.

I went back out into the hall. The noise of the crowd engulfed me. As I went into the girls' room, I smelled cigarette smoke. The girls were comparing notes on their weekend activities. Some of the smokers said that they had gone to church Sunday. As I left the room, I asked myself why would anyone go to church on Sunday and on Monday want to brag about it over a cigarette?

I thought about how lucky I was to live in this country and to possess so many benefits and to have a Christian faith that meant so much to me. I wondered sometimes if I was really the handicapped person.

The morning went fast and at last I had English. I loved English, and I was glad when that period finally arrived. We were studying Macbeth and I was getting very involved in it. I listened to my teacher eagerly as I tried to take notes. My fingers moved stiffly and I couldn't write fast. Mr. Dell was talking about Lady Macbeth's role in the play.

"Don't you think she was trying to get a good name for herself?" I asked excitedly.

"I'm sorry, Kathy," my teacher said, "we didn't hear all of that."

I hated to repeat, and I was very embarrassed. I told myself to try harder, talk slower, and not to worry about it, but I still felt bad. And yet, I thought, God must have a plan for me.

I went to lunch, still thinking about my teacher's views on Macbeth. The cafeteria was crowded and people scurried from one place to another. I got my lunch and carried my tray to a table.

Then I heard voices and laughter behind me. "Have you ever seen her eat?" I looked at the boy who was talking. "She fell yesterday and I nearly died laughing."

"Yeah, and she thinks that everybody likes her," his girlfriend replied. They laughed again.

I tried to tell myself that they weren't talking about me, but I knew they were. "Love those who hurt you," I thought as I walked through the halls. Can I really do that?

I went to visit Mr. Dell. "Hello, Mr. Dell." I tried to sound as if nothing had happened.

"Well, Kathy, I really liked that essay you wrote." Mr. Dell always smiled.

"Gee, really?" I loved it when he complimented me.

"Yes, you have a great deal of potential in the field of English."

I was thrilled to hear him say that.

"You'll do well in college English, and I want you to keep up your interest in it. You may even turn out to be a dumb teacher like me." We both laughed.

I started walking to my locker. Yes, maybe I will turn out to be a teacher, I thought. Those kids in the cafeteria didn't really matter now. I had to go on. I had to prove to them, and even more to myself, that God had a plan for my life. I knew that all the things that happened today would happen again, and I knew that I would have to face them again. Yet, I knew, too, that God would always give me strength.

When does my faith mean most to me? Why, every single day.

Danita Cash

The Longest Walk of My Life

It was a beautiful sunny day in April as I drove down the country road to the woods where my brother Randall and his friend were target practicing. I slowed to a stop before the bridge where I was to meet the boys. There was a barricade across the bridge entrance; it was closed to traffic. I honked the horn three times, the signal for the boys to come out to the car. But no one came.

It was quiet. The roads and the woods seemed empty. I honked several times more. And then, as if from nowhere, a man appeared in the road and came toward my car.

My heart stopped. Those were uneasy days in our part of Texas. The recent murder of a young girl exactly my age was still fresh in my mind. And there had been still other murders of young people before that. The killer, or killers, were still at large.

Perhaps that's why I was frightened by the stranger more than I might have been, even though I knew I was safe, that he couldn't get into the car. Besides, Randy would show up soon.

I rolled down my window just a little to talk to him. Before he could say anything I said, "I am waiting for someone. Have you seen two boys here with guns?"

"No," he answered. "I've been here an hour and I haven't seen anyone." I told him that if he saw them to please tell them that I was waiting.

"Okay," he said, and left, walking toward the bridge.

I sat there thinking that maybe I should leave, but I knew Randy and his friend would appear any minute. I was still not at ease, but I thought to myself, *Nothing is going to happen.*

Suddenly the man, who had been on the bridge, started walking back toward my car, this time carrying a shotgun at his side. *He's coming to tell me where they are,* I thought.

But when he reached the car he raised the gun to the window. "Unlock the door," he said.

I couldn't believe it. I thought I must be dreaming.

"No," I said.

That made him mad. "Open it!" he demanded angrily. "This gun can shoot through the door." So I unlocked the door. He told me to move over.

I began to realize what was happening to me and I wanted to cry and scream, but fear prevented anything from coming out. The man took out a piece of wire and bound my hands behind my back, then told me to get out. Many thoughts raced through my mind. I had a tremendous ache in my heart for mom and dad. They would never know what had happened to me or where to begin looking for me. Yet despite my fears, I knew that God was near me. I knew he loved me and wanted the best for me.

"When I am afraid, I will trust in you" (Psalm 56:3) raced through my mind. I thought how all my life I'd heard, "Put your trust in God. He will take care of you." I had always had faith in God, but this, I knew, was the big test.

"Oh, God," I prayed, "I know in my heart that you are going to take care of me and that I shouldn't be afraid. I thank you for whatever is going to happen to me." I felt calm then, knowing God was there with me.

Across the long, barricaded bridge I could see a blue-and-white pickup truck. As we walked toward it, with the gun pointed at me, the man grabbed my arm. I stopped still. "I won't take another step," I said firmly, "unless you remove your hand." His hand dropped and we continued walking. I was praying silently with every step.

When we reached the truck, he pushed me inside. He got a roll of white tape and wrapped it around my head, mouth and nose three times. Then he went around the truck and got in. He noticed a car approaching in the distance so he pushed me to the floor board. I kept rising and he kept pushing me down.

But I continued to turn to God for his protection. I knew that God was going to take care of me. I did not know how or when, only that he would do it in his own special way.

The man started the motor and hurriedly backed down the road. He backed up to quite a distance from the bridge. I tried to speak, letting him know that it was hard for me to breathe. He reached over to adjust the tape and when he did, he lost control of the truck. It slid into a ditch and sank into the mud. And his door would not open because of the embankment.

Angrily he crawled out on my side and said, "Look what you made me do." After viewing the situation, he crawled back into the driver's seat and tried again to free the stalled truck, but to no avail. He took the tape off my mouth. "Please let me go," I said.

"Sure," he said, "and the first thing you'll do is go to the police. You know my face and license number."

"No. No," I argued. "I didn't even look at your license number."

It was then that I began talking to him about Jesus. I told him I was a Christian. Showing him my necklace, a cross superimposed on the sign of the fish, I said, "This doesn't prove I'm a Christian, but it is a symbol of my faith. Nearly all my life I have been a Christian. I believe in my heart that Jesus died on the cross for me." He kept looking at me as I talked, really listening to everything I was saying.

"I've never trusted anyone in my life," he said when I was finished. Then he freed my hands and said, "Walk all the way back to your car, not saying a word to anyone. If you run I'll shoot you."

That was the longest walk of my life. I was running on the inside, but outwardly I walked all the way back and got into my car. While driving home I kept repeating over and over a prayer of thanksgiving. "Thank You, God. Thank You, God, for delivering me."

My mother called the police and our pastor. A couple of weeks later the man was apprehended. He not only confessed to kidnapping me, but confessed to three murders he had committed. This convinced me all the more that God had truly worked a miracle in my life. He gave me a calmness that I needed so that I was able to share my faith.

The day after it all happened I remember looking out the window at home and telling mother, "It's like a brand new world. The grass is so green, the sky is so blue, the sun is so bright. Life is so wonderful and so very precious to me."

That experience brought me closer to God than I have ever been in my life. He guarded and guided me through a dark and frightening time, just as the Bible promises in Psalm 23: "Even though I walk through the valley of the shadow of death, I will fear no evil, for you are with me." Truly I know that God was with me, and that he will always be with me through all my life.

Barry Alfonso

The Friend I Didn't Want to Have

*I*t *was* the first day of school and as I waited in the cafeteria lunch line, I looked across the room to see how many familiar faces I could spot. Then I saw a boy with large glasses sitting by himself toward the back, someone I didn't recognize. Curious, I asked a few friends who he was, but they hadn't seen him before either.

After lunch I asked the teacher monitoring the cafeteria about this new kid. She explained that he had just moved to this area and that it would be nice if I tried to make him feel welcome here. She added a bit awkwardly, that he was mentally retarded.

For some reason I felt uncomfortable after asking her. Of course she was right—the kid, whose name was Matthew, was probably lonely and I felt sorry for him. But I didn't want to reach out to him either. It's hard to explain, but I couldn't see him as a real person. Being around him made me feel, well, strange. I felt guilty about it, too, and I tried to put him out of my mind.

I was glad that I didn't have classes with him. I saw him in the school hall every day, going to or leaving the special class that he attended for students with learning handicaps. When I passed him I always noticed that he seemed happy and not at all like the lost, confused child I imagined he must be. He seemed at peace with himself—but I only saw him for a second each day and, anyway, how could I hope to understand a person like Matthew?

I had never spoken to him until the time he came up to me in the school library. I was doing homework when Matthew politely tapped me on the shoulder and asked me to read him something out of a magazine he was holding. He opened it to a page with a photo of a rocket launch on it; the article with it was on space travel and obviously too difficult for him. I couldn't refuse his request, but I didn't enjoy the experience. I was embarrassed. I didn't want any of my friends to see me with this retarded boy. *Why did he have to ask me to read to him?* I thought. I only half heard him thank me when I was through. I was glad to see him leave.

It didn't seem long after school had opened that Christmas vacation came. I had been looking forward to the holiday season for some time—and this year I had a special reason to do so. My Uncle Mark in Florida, a professional watercolor artist who specialized in seascapes, had hinted in his last letter that he might send me a gift. Since he knew how much I loved his work, it could only mean one of his latest paintings. For days I hung around the post office, watching the mail, awaiting that special package.

It finally came a few days before Christmas. I didn't open it, but the package's shape and weight told me that my uncle hadn't disappointed me. By the time I had finished some last-minute holiday shopping and caught a bus for home that evening, I was debating whether to open it then or save my enjoyment until Christmas Day.

Just before I got off at my stop, I spotted Matthew sitting by a window in another part of the bus. I was going to say hello to him, to wish him a happy holiday. *But why bother,* I thought. *It won't mean anything to him.*

When I arrived home I put down my packages and then something struck me—my gift wasn't there! I was frantic. Did I leave it in a store? Or on the bus? I called all the shops that I had visited that were still open, but they hadn't seen it. My leaving it on the bus seemed more and more likely. If that had happened, it was probably gone for good. I felt terrible.

The next morning as I was preparing to set out to search for the present the phone rang. It was a woman my mother knew calling, but she asked for me.

"There's a boy down at my house who says he's looking for you. Do you know him? His name's Matthew. . . ."

I said I did. I was about to tell her that I had to be leaving when she told me something that made me almost drop the phone.

"Matthew has a package with him. He says it's yours. I'll drive him over if you'd like."

"Yes, that would be fine," I managed to murmur. I was still stunned when I put down the receiver. I realized that I had in fact left the present on the bus. I also realized I was thinking over other things, too—and they made me feel very ashamed.

There were so many things I wanted to tell Matthew when he arrived. I realized now that it wasn't Matthew who was lacking, but me. He wasn't the one to be pitied. I was, because of my narrow-mindedness. But when I showed him in and thanked him, the words just didn't come. I didn't need them anyway; I think he understood.

"You left this on the bus yesterday," he said. "I thought you wanted it." He explained how he had found it under my seat, then rode the bus again this morning to my stop and went looking for me on foot from there, asking anybody he met where I lived. His speech sounded so much clearer than the time he had spoken to me in the library—or maybe I was just listening better now.

I tried to pay him a reward, but he wouldn't accept anything. He told me that his ride was waiting and he had to go. As he stepped outside, he turned and wished me a merry Christmas. I could only wish the same to him. I was too humbled to add anything else. As I closed the door my eyes were welling over.

I don't know where Matthew is today. His family moved out of town a few months after he returned the gift to me. But I know wherever he may be, he is still the same beautiful person. For what Matthew had inside—an honest, beautiful kind of love—could not be taught in a classroom, because it was born in him.

And he possesses a truth that he will share readily with anyone who will accept it—the truth of kindness. Matthew, the handicapped boy I once felt sorry for, taught me that even in the face of ignorance and misunderstanding, love can emerge. It's a rare and wonderful kind of knowledge.